MADE IN SHROPSHIRE

Inspiring recipes using the very best Shropshire produce

Photopia Photography

Made in Shropshire
www.recipesmadehere.co.uk
Published by Photopia Photography, Copyright © Photopia Photography.
www.photopiaphotography.co.uk
First published 2015

Design and layout: p and r design
www.pandrdesign.com

Editor: Jo Hilditch
www.britishcassis.co.uk

Project manager: Beth Heath
www.bethheathevents.co.uk

Illustrations: Mister Charlesworth
www.mrcharlesworthdesign.com

Print: Orphans Press Ltd
www.orphans.co.uk

ISBN 978-0-9927021-1-3

With love & great expectations
Andrew, Alison, Tim, Iain
Doug & Millie
Christmas 2015

Foreword

By Beth Heath, Shropshire Food Ambassador

The landscape is stunning; Shropshire is part-county and part-paradise. It boasts an Area of Outstanding Natural Beauty, dramatic hills and idyllic rolling fields. They change with the seasons: bursting with life in spring, shimmering through lazy, hazy summers before the onset of artistic autumnal colour and the harsh bite of winter.

Each day, hundreds of men, women and children take their workplace in this magnificent countryside. They tend the land; raise crops, rear livestock and harvest nature's rich bounty. Sharing their passion in kitchens, sheds and small units they produce artisan food that travels from farm to fork right here in this picturesque county that so many of us call home.

It is against this scenic and productive backdrop that I have made my living and taken my inspiration. Shropshire's farmers, food producers, chefs and restaurateurs are my friends as well as my colleagues, and it is their work that is celebrated in this striking volume, Made In Shropshire.

My career so far has taken me from working behind the counter of Green Fields Farm Shop to sitting on the board of Ludlow Food Festival; representing the county as their food ambassador, running my events company and the enormously popular Shrewsbury Food Festival with more foodie events to come.

Each day I'm privileged to observe at close quarters the love and respect those local producers and chefs confer on the food and drink of Shropshire. I learn about the patience and skill that it takes to make some of Britain's greatest food. And, best of all, I get to taste the fruits of their labours!

In the past two decades, Shropshire has emerged as one of the UK's most important counties for food and drink. It has enjoyed a surge of popularity as people from all corners of the globe have descended to learn more about the delicious products to be found in our region. Visitors and locals have tasted the incredible and often unique flavours that make our county stand out from the rest. They have dined in exquisite restaurants and enjoyed the skills of the regions best chefs.

The county's chefs and producers are celebrated right here, in Made in Shropshire. So whether a chef, producer, cook or farmer within these pages you will find the raw passion of hopes and dreams; share stories and experience a rare insight to what makes their food so special. And, of course you will have the opportunity of recreating their recipes and producing fabulous great tasting dishes at home.

I've been fortunate to make a career in the county I am proud to call home, I relish each day and look forward to what it holds. You can share my passion on these pages and experience for yourself the tastes and textures that make local Shropshire food so special. So turn the pages and tuck right in to enjoy the best of Made In Shropshire!

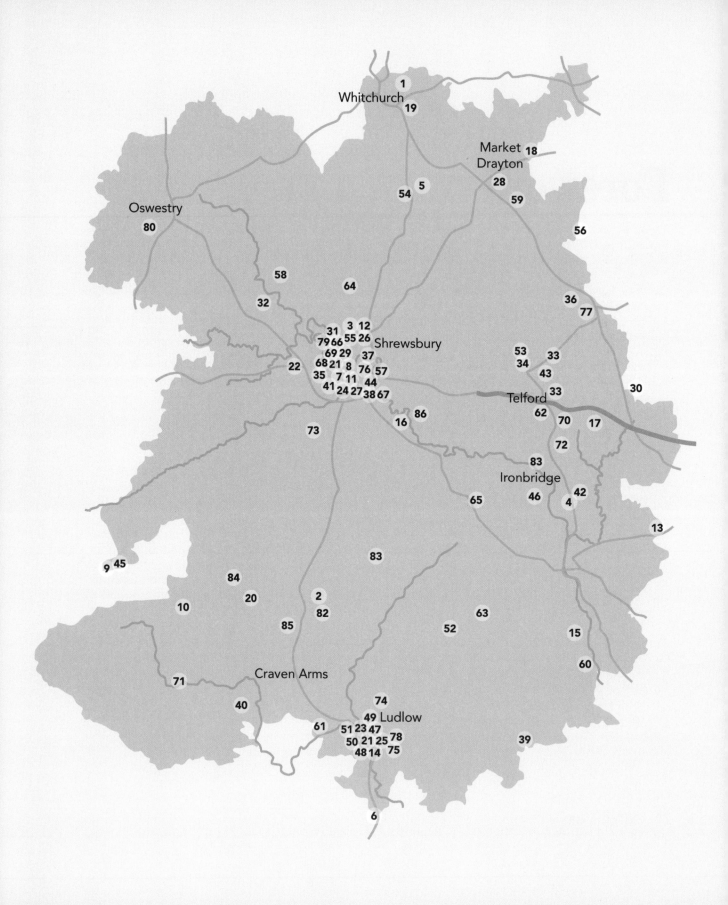

Whitchurch

Market
Drayton

Oswestry

Shrewsbury

Telford

Ironbridge

Craven Arms

Ludlow

Location map

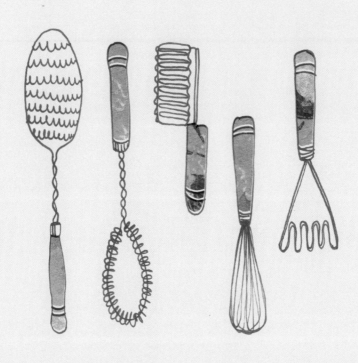

Utensils...

Contents

Scrumptious starters and sensational snacks

Mouthwatering mains

Passionate puddings, naughty nibbles and divine drinks

Scrumptious starters
and sensational snacks

Wenlock Spring Water

Water & ice

"We celebrate our 25th anniversary this year, so a drop in the ocean compared to the history of our spring source. The Wenlock Edge is a geologically famous limestone escarpment created 400 million years ago running from Much Wenlock to Craven Arms. It consists of Silurian limestone which was originally formed in a shallow, warm, clear, subtropical sea, rich in dissolved calcium carbonate and supporting reef building animals, which are found today fossilised within the rock. During the Ice Age this Silurian Limestone was pushed and moved from South of the equator to its new home in South Shropshire. Our water filters through this rock strata providing it with its unique blend of minerals, including calcium and selenium, giving it a refreshing and delicately sweet taste." **Stephen Tuck**

Shropshire Asparagus in a Wenlock Spring Tempura

Served with Truffle and Rapeseed Oil Mayonnaise, Poached Duck Egg and Herb Salad

1 For the mayonnaise, whisk the egg yolks, lemon juice, salt and mustard in a bowl, very slowly drizzle in the oils whisking constantly so that it incorporates fully. It should appear thick and creamy. If it splits add a small drop of hot water and whisk.

2 For the tempura, mix 100g of the self raising flour, with the cornflour, egg. Gradually add in the water, until a light batter consistency is created. Do not over whisk. Toss asparagus in remaining 50g flour, then into the batter. Deep fry at 180°C until golden and crispy.

3 For the duck eggs, bring a pan of water to the boil add the vinegar, swirl the water. Turn down to a simmer, cook each egg individually for 3 mins each, in the middle of the slowly swirling water.

Finally, mix the herbs with drizzle of oil, season and arrange on the plate.

Serves: 4

For the mayonnaise:
- 2 egg yolks (large organic)
- 1 tablespoon freshly squeezed lemon juice
- ¼ teaspoon salt
- ¼ teaspoon Dijon mustard
- 200ml extra virgin rapeseed oil
- 20ml truffle oil

For the Tempura:
- 100g cornflour
- 150g self raising flour
- 330ml Wenlock Edge Sparkling Water, chilled
- 1 egg, beaten
- Salt and pepper
- 12 asparagus spears

For the duck egg and herb salad:
- 4 duck eggs
- 10ml cider vinegar
- 150g mixed herbs, (chives, dill, fennel, sorrel, bittercress, etc. whatever you prefer)
- Drizzle of extra virgin rapeseed oil

The White Hart, Ironbridge

"We are really just 'the new kids on the block' in Shropshire having only opened in April 2014. But we are fast establishing ourselves, with both locals and guests now travelling across the county to seek us out. The White Hart is a relaxed café bar by day and a modern restaurant with a busy cocktail and wine bar in the evenings, all housed in a 16th Century Ironbridge ale house. The food is carefully prepared and a huge amount of work goes into creating each dish; we don't seek to serve big numbers, rather we try to create dinners guests will remember for a while to come" **Alex Nicoll**

Venison Carpaccio, Pickled Beetroot and Candied Walnuts

1 For the carpaccio, toast the seasoning and mix in processor. Spread toasted seasoning mix onto a tray. Roll venison in seasoning mix.

2 Heat a large frying pan add a drizzle of oil. Seal all surface area of meat in hot pan. Remove from heat and allow to cool.

3 Wrap the venison tightly in cling film, roll into a neat cylinder, and pop into the freezer.

4 For the pickled beetroot, bring seasoning to boil and pour over beets and steep.

5 For the candied walnuts, boil sugar and water to syrup, add nuts, boil and coat in syrup, strain and cool. Drain.

To serve… slice carpaccio from freezer, season and arrange on plate. Garnish with walnuts, beets, cheese and chard. Dress with a mustard vinaigrette.

... *beetroot*

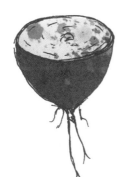

Serves: 6-8

For the carpaccio:
- 1 saddle venison loin, fillet removed, trimmed
- 10g black pepper
- 5g jun
- 5g star anise
- 10g Maldon Sea Salt
- 5g fennel

For the pickled beetroot:
- 300g baby beets, cooked and peeled
- 345g caster sugar
- 750ml white wine vinegar
- 2 quince
- ½ teaspoon cloves
- 2 bay leaves
- 1 tablespoon black peppercorns
- 2 star anise
- Peeled zest of orange

For the candied walnuts:
- 300g walnuts
- 100g caster sugar
- 100ml water

To serve:
- Chard
- Cheese, of your choice
- Mustard vinaigrette

Ludlow Vineyard & Distillery

"Our lives now are rather different to our previous incarnations in accountancy and banking. Owning and operating one of the few craft distilleries in the UK and turning a hobby into a business has been very rewarding. Our Shropshire Applejack (the EU have outlawed the name apple brandy) from the apples in our orchard, and our English vineyard brandy from grapes from our vineyard, are two delicious products that we drink only in strict moderation. Each sip is savoured! And coming soon is our own malt whisky! And, we still know how to balance the books." **Mike and Barbara Hardingham**

Shropshire Applejack Tapas

1 Put the sliced chorizo with the olive oil in a frying pan and fry over a medium heat for until the chorizo is browned and crisped up a bit. Plenty of fat should come out of the chorizo.

2 Add the potato pieces into the pan the and fry for 5-10 mins until they are well cooked and browned. Add the onion and the apple, allow to soften, then add the green or French beans along with the apple juice or cider. Turn the heat down while the beans cook, adding more cider or apple juice (or water) if the pan becomes too dry. The mixture should remain moist but not sloppy.

3 Finally add the Applejack. You can set light to the pan if you wish to burn the alcohol off!

Serve immediately.

Serves: 2
- 125g Shropshire Chorizo from Wenlock Edge Farm, sliced thinly
- 1 tablespoon olive oil
- 350g potatoes, diced into 1cm cubes
- 1 onion, chopped roughly
- 1 dessert apple, e.g. Cox or Braeburn, diced small
- 300g green or French beans (fresh or frozen), chopped as desired
- 50-100ml apple juice or cider (we used Ludlow Apple Press)
- 50ml Shropshire Applejack
- Salt and freshly ground pepper

Wroxeter Roman Vineyard

"English wines are now all the trend and we are part of that new wave, but based next to the very old Roman city of Viriconium. At its peak, Viriconium is estimated to have been the 4th largest Roman settlement in Britain, a civitas with a population of more than 15000. The settlement probably lasted until the end of the 7th century so our 24 year old business is a mere flash in the pan compared with the history of our village – our wines are long lasting too. With 15 varieties we think there is something to suit everyone, even a Roman!" **Amanda Millington**

Ultimate Fennel and Heritage Tomato Salad

1 Cut the fennel into inch thick pieces then cut them in half. Heat a drizzle of oil in a frying pan and brown off the fennel in batches until golden all over. Season with salt and pepper and then add in the wine, sugar and water. Simmer gently until the fennel has become soft, then leave to cool.

2 Cut your tomatoes any which way, the more texture the better! Drizzle with olive oil and sprinkle with salt. Mix in the fennel and the black olives and serve with rocket and toasted ciabatta chunks to soak up the juices!

Serves: 6-8
- 3 fennel bulbs
- A drizzle of olive oil
- Salt and pepper
- 150ml Wroxeter Vineyard Regner White Wine
- 50ml water
- 25g caster sugar
- 500g mixed heritage tomatoes
- 1 handful black olives

Apley Farm Shop

"Situated in the heart of Lord Hamilton's Apley Estate, we are so much more than a farm shop – we are a destination! We opened in 2011 in sympathetically restored farm buildings. Being able to supply our customers with tasty, local and seasonal food and drinks, many of them made in Shropshire, and some coming from our own walled garden is our main focus. There is so much to taste, discover and enjoy at Apley Farm Shop!"
Lady Harriet Hamilton

Martin McKee's Pumpkin Soup
Served with Homemade Soft Granary Rolls

1 For the granary rolls, add both flours, salt and yeast into a bowl and rub together with your finger tips. Make a well in the centre and pour in your water and melted butter, combine together with your hand until you have a soft dough. Lightly flour your work surface and transfer your dough and knead for 10 mins until smooth and elastic. Place your dough into a bowl and cover with a towel, leave in a warm area to prove, your dough should have doubled in size after an hour.

2 Divide your dough into 14 even balls and place close together (but not touching) on a baking tray lined with baking parchment. Sprinkle the tops of your rolls with cracked wheat and ground roast pumpkin seeds. Preheat your oven to 190°C (170°C fan) and bake for 15 mins. Best served warm from the oven.

3 For the pumpkin soup, roughly chop the pumpkin flesh, carrots, potato, shallots, celery and red chilli pepper. Put into a heavy based pot and sweat for 5 mins over a medium heat stirring occasionally.

4 Add the garlic, ginger and nutmeg and stir together. Next add your coconut milk, honey and stock. Bring to the boil and reduce heat to simmer for 50 mins.

5 When your vegetables are soft, blend your soup with a hand blender or food processor. Return to the heat, then add your lemon juice, cream and pepper.

Your delicious soup is now ready to serve. This soup also works great if you substitute the pumpkin for either butternut squash or sweet potato.

Serves: **4**

For the soft granary bread rolls:
- 500g granary bread flour
- 250g unbleached strong white flour
- 1½ teaspoon table salt
- 1 tablespoon dried active yeast
- 400ml warm water (mix 200ml boiled water with 200ml cold)
- 15g unsalted butter, melted
- 1 egg white
- Sprinkle of cracked wheat and roast pumpkin seeds, coarsely ground

For the pumpkin soup:
- 950g pumpkin flesh – keep seeds for roasting (optional)
- 1 large potato, peeled
- 2 carrots
- 4 shallots
- 2 sticks of celery
- 1 red chilli pepper, seeded
- 1 clove of garlic, puréed
- ½ teaspoon fresh ginger, grated
- ½ teaspoon ground nutmeg
- ½ teaspoon ground white pepper
- 150ml coconut milk
- 100ml clear honey
- 1250ml fresh homemade chicken or vegetable stock
- 1 lemon, juiced
- 225ml double cream

Pumpkin ...

Dorrells Restaurant at Hadley Park

"Our beautiful listed grade 2 Georgian manor house has a history of proud and interesting owners, from local industrialists to a Japanese precision instrument company who used it as a haven for their countrymen on visits to the area. As the largest farm in the area it was always the best employer of the village, just as we are now. Still a haven of tranquility near the more populated area of Telford we are proud to use only the best of local produce and to have our expertise recognised through being awarded a coveted Rosette." **Mark Lewis**

Seared Scallops, Pork Belly, Pork Scratchings and Apple Emulsion

1 To prepare the pork belly, sprinkle half the salt in the bottom of a tray and add the belly, skin-side down. Add the rest of the salt on top and rub in well. Cover with cling film and place in the fridge for 12 hours.

2 Heat the oven to 100°C (80°C fan). Wash, dry and then wrap the belly in oven-safe cling film and then in tin foil. Roast for 12 hours. Remove from the oven and carefully remove the skin and set aside to make the scratchings, place another tray on top of the belly and weight down. Leave in the fridge for 24 hours. Remove the tin foil and the cling film and cut into portions.

3 Brown the belly on all sides in a frying pan. Then place in a warm oven at 150°C (130°C fan) until ready to serve.

4 For the pork scratchings, take the skin from the belly removed earlier and cut into 3 inch pieces, then cut into thin matchsticks and place on a tray lined with greaseproof paper, place another piece of greaseproof on the top and another tray to weight down, place in the oven at 180°C (160°C fan) for 15 mins, remove the top tray and paper and place back in the oven and allow to crisp up, set aside on a J-cloth until ready to serve.

5 For the scallops, make sure the scallops are cleaned and stored in the refrigerator on a clean tea towel or J-cloth before cooking. To prepare the scallops, cut each in half to form 2 rounds and season lightly with salt. Place a frying pan over a high heat and add a dash of vegetable oil. Once the pan is almost smoking, add a few of the scallops, making sure you do not overcrowd the pan, as this will cause them to stew and not sear and caramelise. Sear the scallops on each side for 30-45 seconds or until golden brown on each side. Repeat to cook the rest of the scallops.

6 For the apple emulsion, in a non-reactive pan, over low heat, reduce apple juice and cider with star anise, cinnamon and ginger by 75 percent. Strain out solids and pour liquid into a blender. Add vinegar and while blender is running, drizzle in oil. Season with salt and pepper.

Arrange the scallops, pork belly and scratchings carefully on the plates, dot on the apple emulsion and add some delicate herbs to garnish.

Serves: 6-8
- 1kg of pork belly
- 100g sea salt
- Scallops (allowing 3 per person)

For the apple emulsion:
- 475ml apple juice
- 475ml apple cider
- 1 star anise
- 1 cinnamon stick
- 60ml rice wine vinegar
- 120ml pomace oil
- Salt and black pepper

Pig

Granary Grill & Deli at Weston Park

"Weston Park was built in 1671 and is the former ancestral seat of the Earl's of Bradford. Gifted to the nation in 1986 the historic house and grounds are open to the public during the summer months. The Granary Grill and Deli are housed in our beautifully restored 1767 granary building. Previously, you would have seen malt and hops laid out for drying before being taken to the brewery, nowadays you will see all sorts of delicious food to tempt your tastebuds. Although my influence is Mediterranean in style, I can still find wonderful local produce to use throughout the grill and deli." **Guy Day**

Wrekin Blue and Caramelised Pear Tart

1 Start by making your pickled onions, these can be kept in a jar in the fridge for a few weeks. Peel the baby onions. Mix together the vinegar, wine, sugar salt and chilli. Bring a pan of water to the boil and drop in the onions and simmer until tender to the point of a knife, then place in the vinegar mixture, bring to the boil and then cool. Transfer to a Kilner jar (top up with more white wine vinegar if the liquid doesn't cover the onions completely) and store until ready to use.

2 Mix the ingredients for your poaching syrup and place on a low heat. Peel pears, halve and core. Drop the pears into the poaching syrup and simmer until they are tender to the point of a knife. Remove from the syrup and leave to cool.

3 Roll out the puff pastry so that it's about the thickness of a pound coin, cut into discs (small ones for a starter or you can make these larger for a main course or a buffet dish). Prick with a fork all over.

4 Slice the cooled pears into a fan and arrange on top of the pastry, brush with some of the poaching syrup, sprinkle over picked thyme leaves and bake for 15 mins until starting to turn golden. Remove from the oven.

5 Take large-ish pieces of Wrekin Blue and crumble onto the tart, in and around the pear slices. Return to the oven for 2 mins to melt slightly.

Serve each tart with a rocket salad, pickled onions and a drizzle of aged balsamic vinegar.

Serves: 4
- 2 pears
- One block of puff pastry
- Sprig of fresh thyme
- Rocket leaves
- 100g Mr Moyden's Wrekin Blue Cheese
- A drizzle of balsamic vinegar

For the pickled onions:
- 12 baby onions, peeled
- 145ml white wine vinegar
- 145ml white wine,
- 1 teaspoon sugar
- A pinch of salt
- 1 red chilli, chopped

For the poaching syrup:
- 225g sugar
- 1140ml water
- 1 star anise
- 2 bay leaves

Brock Hall Farm Dairy

"Here at Brock Hall Farm we are the only commercial goat's cheese producer in Shropshire and we are proud to make all our cheese by hand. Our entire team is female, as are our goats! Our pedigree Pure Saanen goats are all born on the farm and registered with the British Goat Society. Their lineage can be traced to the first import of Saanens from Switzerland and Holland in the 1920's. We know most of our goats by their bleat and they are all named and recognised as individuals – each with her own character and special place in the herd. We give every one the very best possible care. And we get back what we put in as clean, healthy, happy goats make the best milk enabling us to make the best cheese possible. Our goats are milked twice a day and we work 365 days a year." **Sarah Hampton**

Capra Nouveau, Pickled Apple, Beetroot Carpaccio and Fennel Salad

Much of this wonderful recipe can be made well ahead of time, making this dish a show stopping starter for impromptu dinner parties.

1 For the pickling liquor, bring all the ingredients to boil, simmer gently for 10 mins, leave to infuse overnight.

2 Roast the beets in oven at 200°C (180°C fan), in a baking tray with an inch of water, covered with foil, until soft. This will take approx. 1 hour. While the beets are still warm, rub off the skins and tops. This way you ensure all the flavour remains in the beetroots. Chop into thin slices, or however you prefer. Pour over half of the sieved pickling liquor. NB. This makes more than needed. They will keep for several months in a sealed container

3 For the apples, pour over the remaining half of pickling liquor, cook for 5 mins and then chill. Once again, this makes more than needed but the apples, like the beets, will keep for several months in sealed container.

4 For the fennel oil, poach the fennel herb for 1 minute in boiling water, immediately refresh in iced water. Remove and pat dry. Blend with oil, lemon zest and some salt and pepper.

5 Very finely slice the fennel bulb, drizzle over the lemon juice and season to taste.

6 Toss the salad leaves of your choosing (we used mustard flowers, bronze fennel herb, green fennel herb and mizuna) dressed simply with some Shropshire rapeseed oil and seasoning.

To finish, cube some of the Capra Nouveau, arrange with the beetroot, apple, fennel and salad and drizzle over fennel oil.

Serves: 4-10
- 12 organic local beetroot, whole with tops and tails intact
- 6 eating apples, peeled, cored and cubed
- 1 bulb of fennel
- ½ lemon, juiced
- Salt and pepper
- Salad leaves of your choosing
- Brock Hall Dairy Capra Nouveau goat's cheese (about 30-50g per person)

For the fennel oil:
- Large handful of fresh green fennel herb
- 100ml of extra virgin Shropshire rapeseed oil
- Zest of 1 lemon
- Seasoning

For the red wine pickling liquor:
- 250ml red wine, preferable English
- 250ml red wine vinegar
- 250g brown sugar
- Zest of 2 oranges
- 12 coriander seeds
- 20 fennel seeds
- 4 star anise
- 25 mustard seeds
- 6 peppercorns

Bennett & Dunn Cold Pressed Rapeseed Oil

"Having farmed oil seed rape for many years, we did not set about making our own oil until 2014. Our oil is natural, totally pure, no chemicals and no heat – we just squeeze the oil gently out of the seed and bottle it. The bees that pollinate our rape are based on the farm and we calculate they travel about two miles per day. And why go further when the crop is on your doorstep – much like local food!" **Tracey and Rupert Bennett**

Pickled Fillet of Red Mullet

Served with Red Pepper Salsa, Bacon Crisps and Saffron Mayonnaise

1 Mix the ingredient for the pickling liquor together and heat until combined. Pour over the mullet and leave to cool.

2 For the salsa, add the lime and lemon juice and zest to the diced vegetables, then add the rapeseed oil and mix together. Season with salt to taste.

3 Place the bacon rashers flat on a baking tray and cook in the oven at 160°C (140°C fan) until dry and crispy.

4 For the mayonnaise, whisk the eggs yolks, vinegar, mustard and saffron over a gentle heat, until the egg mix is light and fluffy. Gradually add the rapeseed oil, about a teaspoon at a time, until all is emulsified. Taste and season with salt and white pepper.

To plate, arrange all the elements delicately on the plate, dotting the saffron mayonnaise along with pea purée, fresh tomatoes, beetroot, croutons and delicate herbs to finish the dish.

Serves: 10
- 10 fillets of fresh red mullet
- 10 rashers of smoked streaky bacon

For the pickling liquor:
- 240ml white wine vinegar
- 240ml water
- 480ml white wine
- 3 peppercorns
- 1 bay leaf
- Half a red chilli (no seeds)

For the salsa:
- 1 red onion, finely diced
- Half a cucumber, finely diced
- 3 tomatoes, deseeded and finely diced
- 1 handful of coriander, finely chopped
- 2 red peppers, finely diced
- 2 lemons, zest and juice
- 1 lime, zest and juice
- 960ml Bennett & Dunn Cold Pressed Rapeseed Oil
- Salt

For the saffron mayonnaise:
- 5 free range egg yolks
- 1 cup of white wine vinegar
- Half teaspoon of English mustard
- 1 pinch of saffron
- 720ml tepid Bennett & Dunn Cold Pressed Rapeseed Oil
- Salt and white pepper

rapeseed flower...

Rowlands & Co.

"We are a 4th generation family owned business that has been supplying catering and retail outlets in our distinctive 'red livery' vans throughout Shropshire since 1894. So we are both well established and have the experience to provide the quality and range of goods required by the good folk of our county. We source as many products as possible locally, forging strong bonds with both growers and suppliers to provide the freshest product at the keenest price. In our eyes seasonal products are paramount. We are also always looking for new ways to invest in our business and make use of modern technology." **Peter and Ian Rowlands**

Serves: **4**

- 300g podded broad beans
- 2 tablespoon olive oil, plus extra for drizzling
- 400g cherry tomatoes
- 1 handful mint leaves, roughly chopped
- 2 handfuls spinach leaves
- ½ lemon, juiced
- Salt and freshly ground pepper
- 8 slices rustic sourdough
- 1 garlic clove, peeled
- 100g parmesan cheese, shaved with a peeler

For the salad:
- Assorted micro herbs (we used red amaranth, rocket, red stem radish and chard)
- 50ml rapeseed oil
- 1 garlic clove, minced
- 1 teaspoon Dijon mustard
- 1 teaspoon cider vinegar
- Salt and pepper

Broad Bean Bruschetta
Served with a Micro Herb Salad

1 For the dressing, gently heat the garlic in the oil until just starting to colour, but careful not to colour the garlic too much. Allow to cool (strain, should you wish), then mix with the mustard, vinegar, salt and pepper.

2 Blanch the broad beans in boiling water for 2 mins. Drain into a sieve and hold under running cold water to refresh them. Peel off the outer hard skins. Use a masher to very lightly crush the beans.

3 Heat the oil in a non-stick frying pan until very hot, add the tomatoes and sauté over a high heat until the juices begin to run and caramelise. Add the beans, and sauté for another minute or two. Add the spinach and mint and heat until the spinach has just wilted. Stir in the lemon juice and season to taste.

4 Heat a griddle pan, drizzle the slices of bread with a little oil and toast the bread on both sides, then rub with the garlic clove. Spoon some of the beans mixture over each slice of bread, scatter over the parmesan and drizzle with more olive oil.

Serve with your dressed micro herb salad.

Broad Beans ...

CSONS

"Opened in June 2015 and housed in a listed Tudor building, our restaurant specialises in #locallysourced, but #globallyinspired seasonal food and drink. This is a family affair, we are four brothers, Reuben, Adam, Ben and Josh, surname Crouch – play on words, CSONS! – our restaurant came about as a result our combined 50 years experience in the industry. CSONS is a relaxed, fun and friendly environment that's all about our love of good food, great drink and people!" **The CSONS**

CSONS Chirk Ceviche

Inspired by his love of all things Japanese, including his lady, and being born in Peru this Japanese twist on the Peruvian classic is one of Josh's favourites! The use of local trout from Chirk Farm makes this a CSONS signature dish.

1 Pickle the cucumbers by dissolving the sugar in the vinegar and pouring this mixture over the cucumbers. Leave for a minimum of 2 hours or prepare the day before.

2 Mix together all the ingredients for the curing pickle, leave to infuse for 2 hours.

3 Make the flat breads. Mix all ingredients and knead until glossy and stretchy (about 10 mins) Leave to rest for 30 mins then shape into little balls and roll out into very thin disks about 6 inches wide. Heat a large flat frying pan and place in dough disk. Once it changes from glossy to dull, translucent to opaque, flip it over and then after a few seconds, flip it out directly on to the gas flame. The flames will make the flat bread puff up. Remove it from the heat and cover with a napkin while you make the rest.

4 Drain the curing pickle and make sure you reserve the juice and the solids. In a bowl pour the drained curing juice over the trout and leave for an hour.

5 Mix mayonnaise and wasabi paste to your tastes, set aside. Marinade the beetroot with the sherry vinegar and season.

Plate up! Make sure you don't get too much of the pickling juice on the plate, build up layers of all the ingredients finishing with salad and a sprinkle of coriander.

Serves: 4
- 2 fillets local trout, pin-boned, skin off, thinly sliced
- 1 cooked beetroot, thinly sliced
- 1 teaspoon sherry vinegar
- Salt and freshly ground pepper
- Chopped coriander
- Lane Cottage Salad

For the pickled cucumbers:
- 200ml white wine vinegar
- 80g sugar
- ½ a cucumber, thinly sliced and salted

For the flat bread: (makes 12)
- 175ml warm water
- ½ teaspoon salt
- ½ tablespoon 'zenons' olive oil
- 300g strong white flour
- ½ teaspoon cumin seeds

For the curing pickle:
- 6 limes, juiced
- 2 lemons, juiced
- 1 teaspoon yuzu paste (spicy Japanese paste)
- 1 red chilli, finely sliced
- 1 teaspoon soy
- ½ teaspoon mirin (rice wine)
- 1 red onion, thinly sliced

For the wasabi mayo:
- Mayonnaise
- Wasabi paste (as much or as little as you like!)

Ludlow Food Festival

"Now that the Food Festival is such an established event in the Ludlow calendar it is easy to forget how it all started, way back in 1995. Like many good ideas, it began in a pub, when a small group of people who had businesses in the town were chatting about the proposed plan to build a supermarket on the recently vacated cattle market site, and the detrimental effect it might have on Ludlow's many independent food shops. The decision was made to put on an event to help promote the independent shops and the wealth of small food producers in the surrounding area. That event was grandly called the Ludlow Marches Festival of Food and Drink and took the form of a producers' market in Castle Square on the Sunday and a drinks fair in the College hall. The now world famous sausage trail enticed sausage lovers in and out of all the butcher's shops, and local pubs and restaurants put on special menus. The festival was such a success that it was agreed to repeat it the following year, using the Castle grounds as a stunning setting. The rest, as they say, is history.

The three day September festival, which regularly attracts in excess of 20000 visitors from all over the world, has spawned other events such as the Spring Festival in May, which is a celebration of real ale, local food and classic cars, and in August 600 people take part in the Magnalonga, an 8 mile walk through glorious Shropshire countryside, with frequent stops along the way to enjoy local food and drink. Since that first event all those years ago, it now seems that there are very few towns in Britain which do not have a food festival, but what makes the Ludlow Food Festival special is that it still remains true to its original aim."
The Ludlow Food Festival Team

Warm Salad of Wood Pigeon and Pancetta

1 To make the dressing. In a bowl, whisk together the rapeseed oil, damson vinegar, mustard, honey and pepper. Set aside.

2 Remove the rind from the pancetta. Cut the pancetta into lardons or strips. Slice the crusts off the bread and cut the bread into 1cm cubes. Heat 2 tablespoons of rapeseed oil in a large frying pan and fry the pancetta, stirring, for 3-4 mins until coloured and some of the fat has rendered out. Remove the pancetta with a slotted spoon and keep warm. Add the bread cubes to the pan, adding a little more oil if necessary, and fry, stirring, for a few minutes, until crisp and golden. Set aside with the pancetta to keep warm.

3 Season the pigeon breasts with salt and pepper. Heat 1 tablespoon rapeseed oil in the frying pan and fry the pigeon breasts for 2-3 mins on each side, until browned and cooked through, but still slightly pink in the middle. Transfer to a board.

4 In a large bowl, combine the salad leaves, the lardons and half the dressing. Divide between four plates. Cut the pigeon breasts into thin slices and arrange over the salad. Drizzle over the remaining dressing and scatter the croutons on top.

Serves: 4
- 1 pack Wenlock Edge Pancetta
- 2 slices Swift's the Bakers Sourdough Bread
- 3-4 tablespoons Great Ness Rapeseed Oil, for frying
- 4 Willo Game Pigeon Breasts
- Salt and freshly ground black pepper
- 1 large bag of mixed salad leaves (try to find a mixture which contains strong leaves like raddichio and endive)

For the dressing:
- 6 tablespoons Great Ness Rapeseed Oil
- 1 tablespoon Chilton Damson Vinegar
- 1 teaspoon Ludlow Street Cafe Ludlow Gold Mustard
- 1 teaspoon clear Shropshire honey
- Freshly ground black pepper

The Marketplace at The Raven Hotel

"We conceived the idea of The Marketplace to complement the Raven Hotel at the Much Wenlock Christmas Fair 2014. No two days are the same when it comes to our poplar tartlets as our chef Jason is in constant research and development. Fish is our thing, we personally select our fish at Birmingham Market to ensure we have the very best produce in time for the Marketplace opening. Availability depends on the daily catches but may include varieties such as gurnard, John Dory, mackerel, red mullet, hake, sea bass, salmon, scallops, cod, haddock, tuna and brill." **Team at The Raven**

Fish Pie Tartlet

1 Beat the butter and add eggs one by one until a smooth consistency is reached. Add zest and salt to flour before sieving over the butter, then fold through. Leave pastry to rest in the fridge for 1 hour. Roll out the pastry to a thickness similar to a £1 coin. Using the pastry case as a guide cut out a circle and gently press the pastry into the case, lined with butter and baking parchment. Blind bake for 12-14 mins at 175°C (155°C fan). Remove baking beans and continue to bake for a further 4 mins. Egg wash while hot and allow to cool.

2 For the flamiche mix. Add all ingredients into a bowl and whisk until fully incorporated. Alternatively you could use a blender to ensure salt and pepper is fully dissolved.

3 Peel and boil potatoes until soft. Using a potato ricer prepare mashed potatoes; add butter and seasoning and mix until smooth. Create a layer of potato on the bottom of the tartlet case before adding a small handful of peas. Then add prepped fish to the tartlet and cover with flamiche mix. Bake the tartlets for 15-18 mins at 180°C (160°C fan).

Serves: 10-12
- 300g salted butter
- 4 egg yolks
- 575g "00" flour
- 1 lemon, zested
- Pinch of Salt
- 50ml egg wash (to glaze)

For the flamiche mix:
- 570ml double cream
- 6 egg yolks
- Pinch of Salt
- Good mill of black pepper

For the filling:
- 100g Maris Piper potatoes
- 30g peas
- 100g salmon, skinned, boned and diced
- 100g smoked haddock, skinned, boned and diced
- 50g fresh water prawns, shelled and deveined

Moyden's Handmade Cheese

"Cheese-making can be dated back to around 7000BC and amazingly the process itself has not really changed in those 9000 years! We've only been around for 10 years, so just a microcosm of cheese history. Quality is paramount – our cheeses are made using the raw milk from a single Shropshire herd of Montbeliarde cattle. The first batch of cheese I made was on my kitchen stove using my grandmother's jam kettle. We have come a long way in our 10 year history, now producing 6 different cheeses – like life sometimes hard, sometimes soft, sometimes blue but can be gooey in the middle and best mature! Our cheeses have been developed and named after well-known Shropshire towns and landmarks each with its own story to tell – like our cheese."
Martin and Beth Moyden

Wrekin Salad

1 To smoke the chicken, first make sure you are in a well ventilated area. Using one pan as base place foil in base, and place the smoking chips on top, then put racking across top of the pan, place chicken onto the racking and season, finally use second pan as lid by up turning it. Put over a medium heat for 5-10 mins or until smoke chips begin to create smoke, turn off heat, allow smoke to dissipate, remove top tin (this may be hot and there may be some smoke so be careful). Remove breasts from racking, drizzle with the rapeseed oil and season. Cook skin side down in oven for 20-30 mins at 200°C (180°C fan) until juices are clear or an internal temperature reads 75°C. Chill in the fridge until required.

2 For the dressing, whisk honey, mustard, vinegar, lemon juice and shallots together. Gradually pour in each oil slowly, whisking constantly. Crumble in blue cheese. Season to taste.

3 For the deep-fried cheese, coat the pieces of cheese in the flour, shake off excess. Pop into the beaten egg and ensure they are coated on all sides, then into the breadcrumbs. Pop back into the egg, then finally breadcrumb again, making sure they are completely covered on all sides and corners. Place into the fridge. Heat a pan of the rapeseed oil to 190°C, fry the cheese until golden. Remove and dry on paper towel, season lightly.

4 To finish the salad, chop the pickled walnuts into quarters. Break up the frisee into small leaves. Finely slice the pear. Slice the smoked chicken. Arrange on a plate and drizzle over the dressing. Finally, place on the hot deep-fried Wrekin Blue Cheese.

Serves: 4
- 1 concorde or comice pear
- 1 frisse or curly endive
- 150g pickled walnuts

For the blue cheese dressing:
- 1 teaspoon local honey
- 1 teaspoon Dijon mustard
- 1 tablespoon cider vinegar
- ½ lemon, juiced
- 100ml walnut oil
- 100ml rapeseed oil
- 1 shallot, finely chopped
- 50g Moyden's Wrekin Blue Cheese
- Sea salt
- Freshly ground black pepper

For the deep-fried blue cheese:
- 200g Moyden's Wrekin Blue Cheese, cut into bite-sized pieces
- Plain flour, for dusting
- 1 egg, beaten
- 1 handful of fine white breadcrumbs
- Good quality rapeseed oil, for deep frying
- Salt

For the smoked chicken:
- 2 organic Shropshire chicken breasts
- Rapeseed oil
- Salt and pepper
- Two old pans or roasting tins of equal size
- Wire racking (larger width than the pans)
- Foil
- 30-50g fine smoking chips, we use old whiskey barrel smoking chips

Wrekin Blue Cheese ...

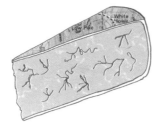

Mikes Homemade

"After hanging up my Executive Head Chef hat in 2008, I set up Mikes Homemade producing homemade chutneys, pickles, preserves, marmalades, mustards and honey. One of my original products was Chilli Jam, which although clearly not a traditional jam, is named so due to the sugar content. My Chilli Jam is packed with natural flavours, infusing red chillies, tomatoes, lemon grass and ginger, the mixture of ingredients creates an aromatic aroma, with a wonderful sweet, tangy, refreshing flavour, with a perfect chilli warmth, it a fantastic cupboard ingredient for marinating, sandwich fillers, glazing or simply with cheese."
Mike Denith

Chilli Jam King Prawns

Served with Rocket Salad on top of Garlic Ciabatta, topped with crumbled Feta Cheese and to finish a drizzle of balsamic glaze

1 Place approx. 1 tablespoon of Chilli Jam, per 4 prawns into a bowl (that can fit easily into your fridge). Add a teaspoon of olive oil per tablespoon of Chilli Jam and stir into the Chilli Jam. Add the king prawns to the Chilli Jam mixture to marinate (ideally marinate for 24 hours, but an hour will suffice).

2 After the marination, place a non-stick pan onto your hob and preheat, adding a teaspoon of olive oil. Once hot, take the marinated prawns out of the fridge and place in pan. Pan fry for approx. 2-3 mins or until cooked through and hot (please note if using chicken, pork or turkey the cooking time will be longer)

3 Prepare your garlic ciabatta. Turn on your grill. Slice 2-3 pieces of ciabatta bread per person (cut the bread so its approx. 1cm thick). Place under grill so lightly browned on both sides. Spread with your garlic butter and place back under grill to melt butter into bread, and remove from the grill.

4 Place a handful of rocket on each plate, top with a sprinkle of small diced red onion and cherry tomatoes cut into quarters. Place the garlic ciabatta on the plate and top with the garlic prawns. Crumble the Feta cheese on top of the prawns.

To finish lightly drizzle balsamic glaze over the whole plate. Did you know you can make your own balsamic glaze by combining balsamic vinegar and sugar and heating until syrupy, then leaving to cool.

Serves: As many people as you have to dinner
- Raw king prawns
- Mikes Homemade Chilli Jam (or Hot Chilli Jam or Jalapeno Chilli Jam)
- Olive oil
- Rocket
- Red onion
- Vine ripe cherry tomatoes
- Feta cheese
- Ciabatta (baguette)
- Garlic butter
- Balsamic glaze

Tip – King prawns can be substituted with chicken, turkey or pork, or if vegetarian, why not mix up chunky chopped mushrooms, aubergine, courgettes, mixed peppers and whole shallots).

Monkfish Cheeks with a Soy Caramel Glaze, Pork Bon Bons and Apple Miso Purée

1 To make the pork bon bons, preheat oven to 120°C (100°C fan). Season pork well with sea salt. Place in oven proof dish. Pour over the stock and apple juice. Foil and cook for 4-6 hours until meat is flaking and tender. Flake down the meat and chill. Once chilled, mould into small spheres and then pané. Tip – to pané is to roll the spheres in flour, then beaten egg followed by the panko breadcrumbs.

2 For the soy caramel glaze, heat an oiled pan and add onion, ginger, and garlic. Sauté for 2 mins. Add water and sugar, bring to a boil. Cook until reduced by half. Remove from heat, whisk in soy sauce and butter. Set aside.

3 For the monkfish cheeks, make a brine by combining the sugar, salt and water in a pan, bring to the boil to dissolve the sugar and salt. Leave to cool. Once the brine is cool, submerge the monkfish in the brine for 10 mins. Pat the cheeks dry and pan fry in a medium-hot oiled pan for 45 seconds to 1 minute on each side, then coat with the soy caramel glaze.

4 For the apple miso purée, sweat the apples in oil for 3 mins. Add the juice, vinegar and wine, boil until you have reduced the liquid by half. Add the miso and sugar. Remove the mixture from heat and stir in the sesame oil, blend until smooth.

This dish is great served with our Viva Vase Vegas cocktail. To make, simply combine 25ml gin, 25ml lychee liquor, 25ml hibiscus liquor, 5ml violet liquor, 12.5ml lemon juice and 12.5ml sugar syrup, stir well, pour over crushed ice, and add edible flowers to garnish.

Serves: 4-6

For the pork bon bons:
- 1kg piece of pork shoulder
- 500ml apple juice
- 1 litre chicken stock
- 100g flour
- 1 egg
- Panko breadcrumbs

For the soy caramel glaze:
- 1 banana shallot
- 5g grated ginger
- 2 garlic cloves minced
- 250ml water
- 125g sugar
- 70ml soy sauce
- 15g butter

For the monkfish cheeks:
- 3 50-75g monkfish cheeks per person
- 400ml water
- 35g sea salt
- 35g sugar

For the apple miso purée:
- 4 granny smith apples, peeled, cored and diced
- 250ml apple juice
- 30ml cider vinegar
- 30g caster sugar
- 125ml white wine
- 20g blonde miso paste
- 10ml sesame oil

House of the Rising Sun

"There is a house in Shrewsbury north, they call the rising sun! Along with my sous chef Liam Watton and our hard working team we have introduced something new to Shrewsbury cuisine – modern Australian cooking with pacific rim flavours along with Indonesian, south American and south east Asian influences – all underpinned by European tradition. Sounds exotic, is delicious and always uses quality local produce."
Sam Butler

Green Fields Farm Shop

"Although farm shops are a relatively new enterprise for many, we have been in this business for over 20 years, selling the very best from our local producers. Connecting farms to the consumer has been paramount – and our twice yearly food festival gives the public an opportunity to engage with the producers themselves. In our richly agrarian county there is so much opportunity for trade and our customers recognise that there's nothing wrong with a dirty carrot – in fact there's everything right!" **Natalie Walker**

Makes: 2 small jars
- 700g Mr Galbraith's dirty carrots, washed and grated
- 1 shallot, finely diced
- Zest of 1 orange
- 150g caster sugar
- 250ml white wine vinegar

Any carrots will work in the recipe, but we think Mr G's are the tastiest around!

Caramelised Carrot Chutney with Mr Galbraith's Dirty Carrots

1 Gently heat the diced shallot with a small amount of oil in a large pan, until soft. Add the grated carrots, orange zest, caster sugar and turn up the heat to medium. Let the sugar caramelise slightly but not colour too much.

2 Pour in the white wine vinegar and bring it to the boil while stirring. Continue to cook until the liquid has evaporated, the carrots are tender and the chutney is a thick consistency.

3 While the chutney is still hot, ladle it into hot, sterilised jars. The chutney will keep for several months. We recommend keeping it at least a month before opening, if you can!

We like ours with Pimhill Organic Oatcakes, Monte Enebro goat's cheese and watercress for a great snack, light lunch or party food.

carrots

Swifts

"Our bakery business was originally started in 1863 by my great, great, great Aunt to support her family after she lost her husband. In the first instance she just supplied her street. My father took on, and continued the baking tradition from his father (great Aunt Hannah's nephew) and they worked together in Field Bakeries during World War 2, based in Mombasa returning home to start a bakery himself. Now, a 6th generation Swift is beginning an apprenticeship in the business this year. Only 4 ingredients are used to make a loaf of our bread and all these ingredients are sourced within 30 miles of our business." **Robert Swift**

Makes: 2 loaves
- 450g Pimhill Wholemeal Flour
- 150g sourdough starter
- 6g salt
- 300ml water, which will probably rise to 350ml

crusty bread...

Shropshire Sourdough

1 Pour your flour into a bowl, work in the salt and add your starter. Add three quarters of your water and begin to work the mixture in the bowl, gently adding your water and mixing, until the dough becomes tacky and sticky. Bring the dough out onto the table and begin to knead. Give your dough three six-minute rests during the mixing process. When you are happy with your dough, oil the bowl, place the dough inside and cover. The proving time in its bulk state should be anything up to 10 hours.

2 If you are making sourdough during the day, put turns and folds onto it every three hours. If you are holding overnight, give it a fermentation of between two and three hours, then turn and fold before covering and placing in the fridge. When you wake up, bring it out, turn and fold, then allow a further two hours fermentation at room temperature.

3 Now flour the table, tip out the dough and divide into two equal parts. Flour your proving baskets, mould the dough into bloomer shapes and place your dough in upside down with the crease facing upwards. Cover and prove for a final time for another two hours.

4 Half an hour before baking, preheat the oven to 220°C (200°C fan) and pop in a baking tray or baking stone. When the tray or stone is very hot, gently turn the bread onto the baking tray and put a single cut into the top of your loaf with your lame. Now put it into the oven with a little steam and bake for 35-40 mins.

Tip – always remember to replace the amount you took out of your starter, and continue to keep up the regular feedings. If you are not using your starter for a prolonged length of time, keep it in the fridge and bring it out the day before to begin feeding again.

Sourdough is a very testing recipe, but once you can master it you can call yourself an advanced baker.

Hopton House B&B

"Our renowned Shropshire Breakfast is one of the reasons our guests return time and time again. Not only this, but the glorious views across the wildflower meadow to the Shropshire Hills in the distance and birds on our nearby garden feeders. In the garden our happy hens range freely, providing us with golden yolked eggs. Our breakfasts have been served for over 10 years and our Eggs Benedict have a special place in the hearts of our guests, along with our blueberry pancakes and full Shropshire breakfast." **Karen Thorne**

Eggs Benedict

This is a very popular special at the B&B and my husband's favourite. If you're cooking for a few people then I suggest you pre-cook the poached eggs and make up the hollandaise and put it in a warmed thermos flask. Then you're only reheating and assembling ingredients when it comes to plating.

1 Start by making the English muffins, mix all the ingredients to a soft dough then knead until the dough is elastic and smooth (or use the dough setting on a bread machine). Leave for an hour in an oiled bowl in a warm place till the dough has doubled in size (or if you're using the bread machine, wait for the ping!). Knock the dough down and split into 8 equal size balls. I then use a large pastry cutter to get 8 circles of dough with straight(ish) sides. Put onto a greased baking tray and cover with oiled cling film. Leave to rise in a warm place for about 30 mins until doubled in size. Preheat a large heavy frying pan on a medium heat, brush with oil, then carefully transfer 2-4 muffins across depending on the size of your pan. Cook for about 10 mins until golden, then flip and cook for another 8-10 mins. These are great eaten warm, but if you leave them to cool, they're best toasted when you're to eat them. They will also freeze very well.

2 For the hollandaise, put the 2 egg yolks in a liquidiser, season with salt and pepper and whizz for a minute. Heat the vinegar and lemon juice together in a small saucepan till just bubbling, then, with the liquidiser running, pour in a slow steady stream over the eggs. Once fully incorporated, whizz for another minute. In the same pan, slowly melt the butter, being careful not to let it burn. Then, with the liquidiser running again, pour the butter in, in a very slow steady thin stream.

3 For the poached eggs, choose your eggs carefully. The eggs need to be as fresh as possible. Also, your poached egg will work much better if you choose an egg from a young hen. If you don't have your own chickens, make sure you buy nice fresh free range eggs. I use my eggs at room temperature. Take a small pan and fill with water. Add a good slug of vinegar. I use ordinary white distilled vinegar. The water needs to be at a fast simmer, so lots of bubbles on the top but not boiling. Break the egg into a small bowl. Stir the water so it's swirling. Don't go mad here or you could just find the egg being dispersed around the pan. Slip the egg quickly into the water and cross your fingers. Simmer for about 3 mins 45 seconds. This will give you just set egg white and a runny yolk.

4 The trick I use to take the stress out of poached eggs is to pre-cook them before I start on the rest of the breakfasts. Take a bowl, fill with water and lots of ice. As soon as your egg is ready, plunge it into the iced water. This means you can prepare all eggs up front then, when the rest of your breakfast is ready, just reheat for a minute in boiling water. Use a slotted spoon to take the egg out, rest on kitchen towel to absorb the water before serving.

And that's it really! Arrange the 2 halves of the English muffin on a plate, place a 2 slices of bacon on each, followed by an egg then the hollandaise. I use chives for a finishing touch. Ta da!

Serves: 6-8
For each serving you'll need:
- 1 English Muffin, toasted and buttered
- 4 slices local bacon, grilled
- 2 poached eggs
- 1 or 2 tablespoons of hollandaise
- Chives for decoration

For the English muffins:
- 1½ teaspoons fast action dried yeast
- 450g extra strong plain bread flour
- 1½ teaspoons salt
- 1½ teaspoons sugar
- 50g soft butter
- 120ml warm milk
- 120ml warm water

For the hollandaise:
- 2 egg yolks
- 1 dessertspoon white wine vinegar
- 1 dessertspoon lemon juice
- 100g butter
- Salt and pepper

For the poached eggs:
- Fresh free range eggs
- 50ml white distilled vinegar

Mouthwatering
mains

Battlefield 1403

"Our farm shop is sited on the battleground of the medieval battle of Shrewsbury – a battle between King Henry IV and a rebellious faction led by the Northumberland Percy family. Founded nearly 600 years after the event and rather more peaceable, our shop is proud to supply products sourced from within 50 miles (where possible) and includes our own beef." **Chris Darlington**

Battlefield's Beef Wellington with Stout Gravy

1 First make the pancakes by whisking the eggs, flour and salt, then whisk in the milk to give a batter consistency. Heat a large frying pan and use it to melt 30g butter, add 1 tablespoon of the melted butter to the batter and whisk. Save the rest of the melted butter to oil the pan between pancakes. Ladle the batter into the hot pan, just enough to thinly coat the surface. Cook until golden then flip and cook the other side. Place onto greaseproof paper and repeat until all the batter is used, using greaseproof paper layers to stack the pancakes.

2 Preheat the oven to 200°C (180°C fan). Brush the beef fillet with a little oil and season with a little salt and pepper. Sear the fillet off quickly in a the hot frying pan, make sure each surface is seared, even the ends. Set the fillet aside to cool slightly.

3 Heat a tablespoon of oil in a pan with 40g of butter, over a medium heat. Add the diced shallots and garlic, and fry gently for about 10 mins to soften. Add the mushrooms and fry, until they go a little dry. Add the chopped thyme leaves, stir and set aside to cool.

4 To assemble, roll out the pastry on a floured surface, to about the thickness of a pound coin. Lay the pancakes evenly over the pastry, then spread the pâté evenly over the pancakes. Spoon over the mushrooms, and place the beef fillet in the centre. Bring the pastry up around the fillet and form a neat parcel. Use the beaten egg yolk to seal the edges, flip onto a baking sheet with the sealed edge at the bottom, and brush the top with the rest of the egg. Score lightly with a knife. Cook for 20 mins for medium rare, a little longer should you wish.

5 While the Wellington is in the oven, make the stout gravy. Melt the butter in the pan you used to cook the meat in. Sprinkle over the flour and stir well. Mix the stock, vinegar and stout together in a jug. Pour half of it into the pan and stir until thickened. Add the rest, let it come to the boil, stirring occasionally until it has thickened. Season with salt and pepper, and add a sprinkle of thyme.

Serve with… seasonal veggies and a bottle of stout!

Serves: **4**

For the pancakes:
- 2 large eggs
- 110g plain flour, sifted
- Pinch of salt
- 275ml milk
- 30g butter

For the mushroom filling:
- 200g chestnut mushrooms, finely chopped
- 2 shallots, finely diced
- 1 clove garlic, finely diced
- 40g butter
- 1 tablespoon rapeseed oil
- 1 large sprig thyme leaves, chopped

For the Wellington:
- 650g Battlefield's Beef Fillet
- A little rapeseed oil
- 75g Battlefield's Chicken Pâté
- 500g puff pastry
- 1 egg yolk, beaten

For the gravy:
- 2 tablespoons butter
- 1 heaped teaspoon flour
- 300ml stout (we used Hobsons)
- 300ml stock
- 150ml red wine vinegar
- ½ teaspoon mixed spice
- 1 teaspoon thyme leaves, finely chopped
- Salt and pepper

Barkworths

"Although not exactly near the sea, we still manage to source the freshest seafood on a daily basis. Indeed, we specialise in 'dayboat' fish that can't be readily found in the supermarkets. Someone once said, "I buy the man, not the fish", in other words, a trustworthy fishmonger is more important than any specific descriptor or designation. Our company is over 100 years old so reputation is important to us and to our customers."
Ian Cornall

Barkworths Saint-Pierre Bouillabaisse

The secret to this great tasting soup is the rich fish stock base. We make our own using whitefish and shellfish bones, combined with the shells of the hundreds of prawns we peel! We add a couple of bayleaves and parsley stalks for great flavour. You can buy our lovely stock frozen, or ask us for any spare bones to make your own.

1 Gently warm the fish stock in a large saucepan. In a sauté pan add a good slug of olive oil, add the garlic, fennel, pepper, leek and onion, cover and sauté over a low heat for a couple of minutes.

2 Deglaze the pan with a glass of white wine, cover again and simmer until vegetable are soft. Add the tinned tomatoes, purée, brown crabmeat and saffron and whizz in a blender (an immersion blender will work too). Add the warm stock and blend.

3 Transfer into a large saucepan and season a little at a time with sea salt and black pepper until you say yum! You will know when the flavours balance, I promise.

4 Pan fry the fish pieces, scallops, and prawns (thickest first) in a little olive oil and rosemary with a sprinkle of seasoning, until lightly browned on the outside. Drop the fish into the warm soup, with the mussels and clams and heat until the fish is cooked through and the shellfish have opened.

Serve with… a dollop of aioli and a sprinkle of parsley. Accompany with torn bread chunks for dipping and a nice bottle of white burgundy.

Serves: 4
- 1 litre fish and shellfish stock
- 1 small fennel bulb, roughly chopped
- ½ red pepper, roughly chopped
- 1 leek, sliced
- 1 onion diced
- 6 garlic cloves, finely chopped
- Olive oil
- 250ml white wine
- 400g tinned chopped tomatoes
- ½ tube tomato purée
- 250g brown crabmeat
- 2 pinches saffron
- Sea salt
- Freshly ground black pepper

- 4 small John Dory fillets
- 4 small gurnard fillets
- 4 cubes hake
- 4 cubes monkfish
- 4 scallops
- 8 peeled raw tiger prawns
- 8 palourdes clams
- 12 mussels

Tip – These are recommendations only, you can use any white fish and shellfish you like (but not oily fish).

mussel

Momo·No·Ki

 *Violets*

"When we opened our new restaurant Momo·No·Ki in July 2014 we were very excited to be bringing authentic Ramen to Shropshire for the first time. Our collaboration with British Lop pig breeder Sam Gray instantly gave rise to many mouth-watering dishes revolving around top quality pork. As a popular ingredient in Asian cuisine the quality of Sam's rare breed pork has allowed us, not only work with a local small farm, but develop dishes with colours and exceptional flavours inspired by the other side of the world. While Sam is one of many local producers to supply Momo·No·Ki and sister-company The Peach Tree, this recipe below represents an excellent example of chef and farmer working together to produce beautiful, and delicious food." **Chris Burt**

52° North aka #FishPigPud

1 Salt and dry pork, refrigerate for 2 hours. Wash off excess salt. Rub with rapeseed oil. Place in preheated 210°C (190°C fan) oven for 15 mins then reduce temp to 160°C (140°C fan) for a further 50 mins. Take out and rest – preferably in a warm place.

2 In a pre-warmed fryer at 180°C add bacon and diced black pudding. After 2 mins remove black pudding and set aside with the pork. Continue to fry bacon until super crisp. Set aside until cool, then place in a food processor until it resembles crumbs.

3 In a food processor blend the edamame to a purée, adding chicken stock until you have a smooth velouté texture.

4 Bring a pan of water to simmer add 1 pack of dashi powder. Blanch the white asparagus, radish, butternut and spring onion.

5 To assemble, warm edamame purée in a pan and add to the plate. Place on the pork and black pudding first. Then cut and place vegetables as desired. Finish with bacon crumb and foraged herbs, leaves and flowers.

Serves: 4

- 400g Middle Farm British Lop belly pork
- 2 tablespoons rapeseed oil
- 200g Maynard's bacon
- 300g Maynard's black pudding, diced
- 250g edamame beans
- A little chicken stock
- 1 pack instant dashi powder
- 10 white asparagus stems
- 4 heritage radishes
- 80g diced butternut squash
- 2 spring onions
- 4 pre-prepared scallops
- Locally foraged, herbs, leaves and flowers

Kerry Vale Vineyard

"We are a small family run vineyard who are passionate about quality, fresh, local, and handcrafted goods. This is conveyed in the care and attention we lavish on our 6000 vines, resulting in beautiful clean tasting wine. This has won us multiple national and international awards and our wines have even been enjoyed in the Houses of Parliament! Our vineyard café and shop exemplifies this philosophy; combining contemporary food and produce with historical points of interest. Although a fairly new vineyard (planted in 2010), the land on which it sits was once home to a Roman Fort, two Roman Marching Camps, a Bronze Age funerary monument and a medieval settlement." **Nadine Roach**

Butternut Squash and Lemon Thyme Risotto

1 Place your pan of stock onto the stove and add the butternut squash, bring to the boil, and then turn down to a simmer. Place the butter, oil, onion and a pinch of salt in a wide pan over medium heat. Cook the onion very gently for about 4-5 mins, until soft but not coloured. It is really important with a risotto not to brown or burn your onion, the bitterness of burned onion would affect the delicate flavours of the dish. Add the leeks and stir. Using a slotted spoon, remove the butternut squash from the stock and add it to the onions and cook for a further 5 mins (leaving the stock in the pan simmering for later).

2 Add the rice and stir very well to coat every grain with the oil. The pan will be getting quite hot and dry now, so add your white wine, sprinkling it in carefully around the pan, this evenly distributes the wine and helps it to reduce and evaporate more quickly. You will hear the wine "singing" as it reduces in the pan. Add half of the lemon juice and half of the zest and cook for 1 minute. Keep stirring gently, the rice will start to look dry again. Now you are ready to add your hot stock, a ladleful at a time. After every ladleful, stir well, really scraping the bottom of the pan, until the stock has almost disappeared into the rice. Then add another ladleful, keeping the rice moist all the time, don't let it get dry in between ladlefuls. After about 15 mins of adding stock and stirring in this way, start to taste, be careful as the rice will be very hot. The rice needs to be tender, but still have some bite to it. Your risotto should take no more than 20-25 mins from start to finish.

3 When you feel that it is almost there, take the pan off the heat and add the peas. Quickly mix in the cheese, and as many picked thyme leaves as you please (saving a sprig or two for garnish). Add the rest of the lemon juice, zest (reserve a little for garnish) and egg yolks, then beat this into your risotto as energetically as you can. The risotto should be nice and relaxed and creamy. If it feels a bit too thick or stodgy, mix in more hot stock a little at a time, until you are happy with the consistency. (Rice retains a lot of heat, so you can relax and not rush to finish it off.) Taste and season if you need to.

Spoon the risotto into bowls, garnish with reserved lemon zest and thyme, enjoy with the remaining 'Shropshire Lady' wine.

Serves: 4
- 1.4 litres vegetable stock
- 1 butternut squash, peeled and diced
- 4 tablespoons butter
- 1 tablespoon olive oil
- 1 large onion, finely diced
- 2 large leeks, sliced
- 400g risotto rice, such as Arborio
- ½ bottle Kerry Vale Vineyard 'Shropshire Lady' Dry White Wine
- 1 medium lemon, zest and juice
- 150g frozen peas
- 85g Parmesan, grated
- Bunch of fresh lemon thyme
- 2 egg yolks
- Sea salt and freshly ground black pepper

Tip for leftover risotto – Using dampened hands, form the cold risotto into little balls. Coat them in fine breadcrumbs, and chill them in the fridge to firm. Heat about 1cm oil in a frying pan. Fry the balls for 5-10 mins, or until crisp and golden on the outside. Drain on kitchen paper and serve with fresh salad leaves for a delicious lunch or snack.

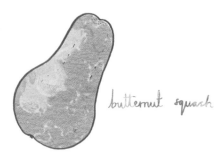

butternut squash

Mediterranean Stuffed Peppers

Served with a Quinoa Rocket Salad and a
Lemon and Lime Dressing

1 To begin with, cook the quinoa according to packet instructions and allow to cool.

2 Slice the tops of the peppers and scoop out the seeds and pith. Wash the peppers, divide the Nutroast mixture into four and fill each pepper.

3 Put 15g of cheese on top of each and replace the tops. Brush peppers lightly with olive oil and bake at 190°C (170°C fan) for 45-50 mins.

4 While peppers are baking, add spring onions and peas to the cooled quinoa. Remove long stalks from the wild rocket, then add it to quinoa with the mint.

5 To prepare lemon and lime dressing, add zest and juice of the lemon and lime, with the sugar, to 3 tablespoons of olive oil, whisk lightly and drizzle over the salad.

We also enjoy this recipe with Romano peppers, sliced lengthways.

Serves: 4

- 2 x 350g Thank Goodness Mediterranean Nutroast
- 8 peppers – orange, yellow and red
- 120g Cheshire cheese
- 150g quinoa
- 450ml water
- 4 spring onions, trimmed and finely sliced
- 100g cooked frozen peas
- A handful of fresh mint leaves, roughly chopped
- 50g wild rocket
- Zest and juice of a lemon and a lime
- 3 tablespoons olive oil (plus extra for brushing)
- 1 level teaspoon of sugar

Thank Goodness

"We create delicious nutroasts, packed with healthy ingredients, that are even praised by our many carnivore customers, who are often very pleasantly surprised by the taste! The nuts and other 'superfoods' in our products have it all in terms of nutrition. Protein, selenium, copper, heart-healthy monounsaturated fats and fatty acids, fibre, antioxidants to name just a few! We started in 2003 with a stall in Newport market, using my partner's mum's scrumptious recipe. Now our nutroasts are sold at various outlets throughout the UK and Ireland. Nutroasts can be used in place of meat in many dishes. This is a wonderfully light and refreshing meal and, using our Mediterranean Nutroast as a filling, could not be easier! Thank goodness!"
Bernadette McCarthy

Great Ness Rapeseed Oil

"Great Ness Farm is situated adjacent to the beautiful Nesscliffe Hill with uninterrupted views across to the surrounding Shropshire Hills. Since 2007 we have been growing, bottling and labelling our award winning and nationally recognised rapeseed oil. Famous for its health benefits of low saturated fat, high in omegas and vitamin E content, it is loved by discerning chefs and cooks alike and recognised for its versatility – ideal in dips, dressings, marinades, baking, stir frying and roasting. With eleven different infusions to choose from, this light delicate and delicious, cold pressed, extra virgin rapeseed oil reflects the splendour of Shropshire." **David Nunn**

Pan Fried Sea Bream

Served with Beetroot Jelly, Fennel Salad and Great Ness Orange Zest Rapeseed Oil Vinaigrette

1 Start by making the beetroot jelly. Place all ingredients except the gelatine, in a pan. Bring to the boil and pass through a fine sieve. Add the gelatine and stir until dissolved. Pour into a container lined with cling film and leave to set.

2 For the fennel salad, mix the sliced fennel with the lemon juice and a pinch of sea salt. Leave in a bowl for 30 mins to marinate. Squeeze the fennel to remove any excess liquid. Place in another bowl and add the chopped chives and the Great Ness Orange Zest Rapeseed Oil and mix well. Season with salt and pepper.

3 For the orange vinaigrette, place the orange juice and zest in a pan and bring to the boil. Reduce this until it becomes like syrup. Whisk in the vinegar then the Great Ness Orange Zest Rapeseed Oil. Transfer to a clean bowl and stir in the diced orange segments.

4 For the fish, heat a non-stick frying pan with Great Ness Orange Rapeseed Oil. When hot, season the fish with salt and pepper and place in the pan, skin side down for 2-3 mins. Turn over the fish and cook for another 30 seconds. Remove from the pan and add a couple of drops of lemon juice.

5 To finish, place the fennel salad in the middle of the plate. Dice the jelly into 1cm square cubes and place 5 jelly cubes around the plate. Lightly warm the vinaigrette in a pan and spoon over the fennel salad and around the plate, then place the fish on top. Garnish with a few sprigs of chervil.

Serves: **2**
- 2 sea bream fillets, scaled and pin bones removed
- 2 tablespoons Great Ness Orange Zest Rapeseed Oil
- Salt and pepper
- Lemon juice
- Chervil

For the beetroot jelly:
- 150ml beetroot juice
- 25g caster sugar
- 25ml ruby port
- ½ star anise
- 25ml red wine vinegar
- ¼ teaspoon mustard seeds
- 2 leaves gelatine soaked

For the fennel salad:
- ½ fennel bulb sliced finely
- Juice from ½ a lemon
- Pinch of sea salt
- 1 tablespoon chopped chives
- 2 tablespoons Great Ness Orange Zest Rapeseed Oil
- Freshly ground black pepper

For the orange vinaigrette:
- 4 oranges – 2 peeled, segmented and diced, 2 zested and juiced
- 50ml white wine vinegar
- 200ml Great Ness Orange Zest Rapeseed Oil

Ludlow Food Centre

"Established since 2007, we pride ourselves on being the epitome of fresh, local, seasonal and handmade food. We are not just a farm shop, we are a food destination! Visitors delight in seeing their food being made by looking through huge windows into the kitchens, whilst they shop. We employ 90 local people who make, serve and promote our great local food. Our 8 production kitchens include a dairy making 11 different cheeses, butter and ice-cream, a butchery that prepares beef, lamb and Gloucester Old Spot Pork from the Centre's estate, a coffee roasting room, a bakery, a jam and pickle kitchen and a production kitchen that makes nearly all the food for the Centre's huge deli. Our lovely site also includes Ludlow Kitchen which serves local, seasonally inspired food and freshly roasted coffee."

Ludlow Food Centre's Shropshire Fidget Pie

1 Make the pastry by sifting the flours and salt into a bowl. Dice the butter and rub into the flour until it resembles breadcrumbs. Stir in the water, a dessert spoon at a time, until the pastry forms a ball. Wrap the pastry in cling film and place in the fridge to rest for 20 mins.

2 Peel the potatoes and cut into chunks and cook in salted boiling water for approx. 20 mins.

3 Cut the gammon into small dice and sauté in a pan for a few minutes until sealed. Add the cider to the pan and simmer for approx. 15 mins until tender. The cider will reduce to a coating consistency.

4 Peel the apples and dice into small chunks, add to the gammon and stir to coat the apples with the sauce, and stir in the sage. Cook for a further 2-3 mins then remove the pan from the heat to cool.

5 Drain the potatoes and mash with the cream, butter and mustard until smooth.

6 Remove pastry from the fridge. Roll out and line a deep 20cm flan dish or 4 individual deep tins. Add the gammon mixture to the pastry case and top with grated cheese. Pipe or spoon the mustard mash on top to create a topping.

7 Place on a baking sheet and bake in a preheated oven at 180°C (160°C fan) for 25 mins. Ensure that the pie is piping hot throughout.

Serves: 4
- 375g Gloucester Old Spot gammon steak
- 2 medium Bramley apples
- 160ml Brook Farm Dry Shropshire Cider
- 750g Shropshire potatoes
- 1 tablespoon Ludlow Food Centre's Wholegrain Mustard with Honey
- 50g butter
- 80g double cream
- 100g Ludlow Food Centre's Oakly Park Cheddar Cheese
- 2 teaspoons chopped fresh sage

For the short crust pastry:
- 75g plain flour
- 75g self raising flour
- 75g butter
- Pinch of salt
- Cold water (to mix)

potatoes

Bistro 7 of Ludlow

"This is our seventh catering business and we established our restaurant in the old Post Office at 7 Corve Street, in the medieval market town of Ludlow – hence the name. Our menus are only guides; if there is something you would like just ask and if we can do it, we will. We always aim to serve beautiful homemade food from the finest ingredients we can source, so instead of putting on our menus "homemade this" and "homemade that"… everything is. Our philosophy is simple; smile, buy great produce locally, cook it well and never say no!" **James and Beverley Croft-Moss**

Braised Shoulder of Mutton wrapped in Parma Ham

1 Cut the mutton into 6 pieces, season with salt pepper and fennel seeds, brown in a frying pan in a little oil. Into a deep dish Slice the carrots and onion add the bones place the browned mutton on top slice the garlic sprinkle on the mutton pour in the wine add the bay leaf, thyme and rosemary. Cover the dish with foil, cook in the oven for about 3-4 hours at 180°C (160°C fan).

2 When cooked take the mutton out of the pan and leave to cool for half an hour. Strain the remaining liquid into a saucepan, leave to cool then put into the fridge.

3 Once the mutton is cool, take off any excess fat. Place a sheet of cling film, approx. 30cm, on the table. Lay two slices of Parma ham on the cling film and place a piece of mutton on top. Now roll the Parma ham and cling film over the mutton to form a sausage shape, hold the edges and draw the sausage towards you so the meat tightens, repeat process for the rest of the mutton. Now chill the mutton overnight.

4 To make the sauce, take the reserved cooking juice and skim off the fat. Slice the onions heat in a saucepan with the vinegar and sugar until soft on a low heat, add the meat juices and the gravy, bring to the boil then simmer for 10 mins.

5 To reheat the mutton, take off the cling film, put into the sauce and either simmer for 20 mins or transfer to the oven at 190°C (170°C fan) for 30 mins. Serve with braised red cabbage and potatoes of your choice.

Serves: 6
- 1 boned shoulder of mutton
- 1 teaspoon of fennel seeds
- 2 carrots
- 1 large onion
- 2 garlic cloves
- 1 bay leaf
- 1 sprig of thyme
- 1 sprig of rosemary
- 1 bottle red wine
- 12 slices of Parma ham
- Salt and pepper

For the sauce:
- 570ml gravy
- 2 red onions
- 1 tablespoon balsamic vinegar
- 1 tablespoon sugar

onion

Brompton Cookery School

"We are based on the stunning National Trust Attingham estate. My wife, Jenny, and I run our unique cookery school in a beautiful barn conversion, it is great place for cookery enthusiasts of all levels to develop their skills and learn some fantastic recipes using local produce and seasonal ingredients. We also run a farmhouse B&B on site too. Recently, we have been working with local artisans Gill and Jon from Sytch Farm Studios. Gill uses British clay for her beautiful handmade bowls and Jon uses local wood for his boards. They create unique items that allow the food and what it's served on to work in perfect harmony." **Marcus Bean**

Serves: 4
- 600g chicken breasts
- 300g slow roast tomatoes
- 1 white onion cut into quarters
- 2 cloves garlic
- 2 thyme sprigs, leaves picked
- 2 teaspoons truffle oil
- 2 tablespoons breadcrumbs
- 2 teaspoons Worcestershire sauce
- ½ teaspoon Tabasco
- 1 tablespoon olive oil
- Sea salt and pepper
- 4 good quality freshly baked bread buns

For the watercress pesto mayonnaise:
- 100g fresh watercress
- 25g parmesan grated
- 25g pine nuts or hazelnuts
- 1 clove garlic, crushed
- 100ml extra virgin olive oil or rapeseed oil
- 4 tablespoons mayonnaise

Chicken and Slow Roast Tomato Burgers with Watercress Pesto Mayonnaise

1 You can make your watercress pesto mayonnaise ahead of time. Add the watercress, parmesan, nuts, garlic and oil into a blender and pulse until just combined. Stir the pesto into the mayonnaise.

2 Preheat a griddle pan on a medium heat and add the olive oil. Put the chicken breast in a blender with slow roast tomatoes, garlic, onion, thyme, truffle oil, breadcrumbs, Worcestershire sauce, Tabasco and blitz until combined. Season with salt and pepper.

3 Once mixed and finely blitzed, remove and shape the mix into 4 burgers, use a pastry ring to make the burgers perfectly round.

4 Once shaped carefully, lift into the griddle pan and cook for about 3 mins on each side until white in the middle and cooked all the way through.

5 Once cooked remove from the pan and rest for 1 minute, slice your bread buns, layer a spoonful of pesto mayonnaise on to the inside of the top bun, place the burger on the bottom, garnish with some fresh watercress or rocket and put the top on.

Serve with… sweet potato wedges or homemade chips, and extra pesto mayonnaise.

Watercress

Masala Magic

"Having worked as an accountant for many years, you can be assured that I will always get the ratios right in all my recipes. However, not many accountants will be able to create a versatile curry masala, korma, tikka, rogan josh and jalfrezi curry like me. Bringing all my skills together means that I can share my spice blends with you online or in my cooking classes which I run with children, adults and corporate team building events. My Curry Masala is a versatile spice blend, it has the base flavours of a Northern Punjabi style curry, with a hint of heat, it's simply Magic!" Lajina Leal

Masala Magic Mixed Vegetable Curry with Cashew Nuts

1 For the yoghurt and mint raita, put all the ingredients, except the yoghurt into a food processor and mix to a pulp, add the yoghurt and pulse again. Serve chilled. For a spicy note, please add a chilli.

2 For the tamarind chutney, put all the ingredients into a food processor and blitz together, you may need to add extra orange juice to get a pleasing consistency.

3 Heat the oil in a big pan, add the onion and fry on a medium heat for 7 mins until golden. Watch they do not stick – if they dry out, add a splash of water. Add the salt and cook for a further 2 mins, before adding all the Lajina's Curry Masala Spice Mix. Sizzle this mix on a high heat for 2 mins, if dry, add a splash of water.

4 Add the tomatoes and cook for 2 mins before adding the potatoes and carrots, pour in half a cup of water, cover and simmer for 7 mins until the potatoes are slightly softened. Add the cauliflower, broccoli, peppers, red onion and cashews and simmer for a further 8 mins until the vegetables are tender.

5 For the chapatis, place the flour into a bowl and start adding a little water at a time, mixing with your hands until you form a soft dough. Knead for a few minutes and cover. Let the dough relax for 10-15 mins. Break off golf ball size amounts, shape into a ball, flatten and roll into a round(ish) shape about 15cm in diameter. Dust off the excess flour. Put the chapati on a hot frying pan and cook the first side for 30 seconds and flip over and cook the second side for a minute and turn over to finish cooking. The chapatis only take 3-4 mins to cook so please watch them.

Finish the curry with a sprinkle of fresh coriander, and serve the curry, chapatis, raita and chutney with a colourful salad.

coriander

Serves: 4
- 1 tablespoon sunflower oil
- 1 medium onion, chopped
- 1 red onion, finely sliced
- ½ teaspoon salt
- 1 pot of Lajina's Curry Masala Spice Mix
- 2 medium chopped tomatoes
- 2 potatoes, peeled and cubed into 3cm chunks
- 2 medium carrots, sliced
- ½ head cauliflower florets
- 1 small head broccoli florets
- 1 red pepper, sliced
- 1 handful of cashew nuts (optional)
- A handful of fresh coriander leaves

For the yoghurt and mint raita:
- A handful of fresh washed coriander, mint and spinach leaves
- ½ teaspoon garam masala
- A pinch of sugar
- A pinch of salt
- 200g Greek yoghurt

For the tamarind chutney:
- 4 tablespoons tamarind sauce (or 1 tablespoon tamarind paste)
- 2 fresh salad tomatoes
- A squeeze of lemon juice
- A fresh chilli
- ½ onion, chopped
- ½ fresh orange, juiced
- 1 tablespoon fresh coriander, mint and spinach (optional)
- ½ apple
- ½ carrot, chopped
- ½ teaspoon freshly roast and ground cumin seeds
- 1 teaspoon sugar
- ½ teaspoon salt

For the easy peasy, cheats chapatis:
- 240g (2 cups) whole wheat or chapati flour, plus extra for dusting
- 235ml (1 cup) warm water

Chef in the Wood

"Our Pop-Up Kitchen was designed and hand built by my dad and me. Our food is all handmade and I recreate traditional recipes, often using the 'Nose to Tail' method of cooking. This is the thrifty rural British tradition of making a delicious virtue of using every part of the animal – well, almost every!" **Ben Foulger**

Braised Venison and Mushroom Stew

Served with Hunters Salami and Herb Dumplings

1 Preheat the oven to 180°C (160°C fan). Heat the oil and butter in an ovenproof casserole dish and fry the venison until browned on all sides. Sprinkle over the flour and cook for a further 2-3 mins. Add the garlic and all the vegetables and fry for 1-2 mins.

2 Stir in the wine, stock and herbs, then add the Worcestershire sauce to taste. Season with salt and freshly ground black pepper. Cover with a lid, transfer to the oven and cook for about two hours, or until the meat is tender.

3 For the dumplings, dice the Hunters salami into small pieces (as small as possible) and cook off in a frying pan and put to one side to cool.

4 Sift the flour and salt into a bowl. Add the suet, flour, cooled salami, chopped parsley, and enough water to form a thick dough. With floured hands, roll the dough into 8 balls.

5 After two hours, remove the lid from the stew and place the dumpling balls on top. Cover, return to the oven and cook for a further 20 mins, or until the dumplings have swollen and are tender, then remove the lid and return to the oven until the dumplings are crisp and golden.

Serves: 4

For the venison stew:
- 2 tablespoon olive oil
- 25g butter
- 750g venison stewing steak, chopped into bite-sized pieces
- 2 tablespoons plain flour
- 3 garlic cloves, crushed
- 175g baby onions peeled
- 150g celery, cut into large chunks
- 400g wild mushrooms
- 200ml red wine
- 500ml beef stock
- 3 fresh bay leaves
- 1 tablespoon fresh thyme
- Worcestershire sauce, to taste
- Salt and freshly ground black pepper

For the dumplings:
- 200g self raising flour
- 100g beef suet
- 60g Hunters salami
- 2 tablespoons chopped parsley
- Pinch of salt
- Water, to make a thick dough

The Happy Boho

 *beetroot*

"We are probably one of the youngest businesses in the book, just launching. Our food blog is based on a happy healthy attitude towards food; one that salads, cake and eating out are all part of. To nourish and energise our bodies we need to eat whole, fresh, real foods and stop obsessing about fad diets and depriving ourselves. All my ingredients are bought from local suppliers and producers. When eating out we highlight the wonderful and local cafés and restaurants that source local ingredients from the farms, markets and great businesses in our county. To enjoy food is to eat happy and love local!" **Annie Hambley**

Happy Ayurvedic Salad

The Ayurvedic philosophy identifies six tastes: sweet, sour, salty, bitter, pungent and astringent. Each taste has different energetic effects on the mind and body, eating the right balance of these foods (which have also been chosen for their high nutritional benefits and mood boosting properties) will help maintain a healthy, harmonious and happy life.

1 Start the happiness, by activating the seaweed in a bowl of warm water for 10 mins.

2 Using a pestle and mortar or a food processor mix together your pesto ingredients to make a smooth paste.

3 Place the kale in a large mixing bowl, then add the pesto and massage into the leaves until they start to soften.

4 Remove the seaweed from the bowl and blot, then add to the mixing bowl with the quinoa, sun dried tomatoes, avocado and edamame beans and mix in well with the pesto.

5 Add a good sized serving to 2 bowls. Thinly slice the beetroot and place round the edges.

6 Melt a little coconut oil in a wok and add the shitake mushrooms and some garlic and cook lightly then divide between the 2 bowls drizzling the leftover coconut oil over the top.

Serve with… sesame seeds, cashew nuts, pomegranate seeds, amaranth and lots of happiness.

Serves: 2
- 2 sheets of nori seaweed
- 3 large handfuls kale
- 250g cooked quinoa
- 150g edamame beans
- 25g sun dried tomatoes
- 1 avocado
- 100g shitake mushrooms
- 1 beetroot
- 1 pomegranate
- Amaranth grains
- Sunflower seeds
- Cashews
- 2 tablespoons coconut oil (coconut oil has incredible immune boosting properties and is antibacterial. It retains these when being cooked at high heat, unlike olive oil)

For the pesto:
- 1 tablespoon tahini
- 1 lemon, juiced
- A large handful of basil
- 1 tablespoon pine nuts
- 1 or 2 garlic cloves

Maynard's Farm Bacon

"Although our business is now 26 years old, we took it on 14 years ago from Maynard Davies (the last of the "Master Bacon Curers") and we have gone from strength to strength. Aside from having a family since we have been here we have also developed a farm shop full of local and artisan products, and become a Rick Stein Super Food Hero. We dry cure our bacon by hand and some of recipes are up to 200 years old."
Rob and Fiona Cunningham

Serves: 4-6
- 1 tablespoon olive oil
- 700g skinless, boneless pork shoulder
- 100g cooking chorizo, sliced
- 1 large red onion, chopped
- 1 large carrot, finely chopped
- 1 teaspoon fennel seed
- Small pinch dried chilli flakes
- 2 garlic cloves
- 4 bay leaves
- A sprig of thyme
- A large pinch golden caster sugar
- 1 tablespoon tomato purée
- 1 teaspoon of smoked paprika
- 50ml sherry vinegar
- 400g tin chopped tomatoes
- 400g tin butter beans, rinsed

For the gremolata:
- 2 lemon, zest only, grated
- 1 garlic clove, thinly chopped
- 2 tablespoons thinly chopped parsley
- 1 teaspoon pink peppercorns
- ½ teaspoon sea salt

Pork, Butter Bean, and Chorizo Hot Pot

This delicious casserole makes an ideal bowl food for crowds. Easy to eat with just a fork!

1 Heat the oven to 160°C (140°C fan). Cut the pork into bite-sized cubes. Heat the oil in a casserole dish with a lid and brown the pork on all sides in small batches. Remove the pork with a slotted spoon and set aside then add the chorizo and sizzle for a minute. Add the vegetables, fennel seeds, chilli flakes, garlic and herbs, and smoked paprika and cook for about 5 mins until the vegetables are soft and just starting to colour. Sprinkle over the sugar and stir in the tomato purée then splash in the vinegar and bubble for a moment. Tip in the tomatoes and a can of water. Stir the pork and juices into the sauce, season with salt and pepper and bring to a simmer.

2 Cover the dish with a lid and place in the oven for 1 hour 45 mins, checking occasionally and if the sauce becomes too thick add a splash more water. Remove the pan from the oven, stir in the butter beans and return to the oven for 15 mins.

3 Gremalata is really simple, and tastes better than the sum of its parts. All you have to do is mix all the ingredients together.

Ladle the stew into warmed bowls and top with a spoon of crème fraîche followed by a teaspoon of the gremolata and a hunk of crusty granary bread to mop up the juices.

Heather's Harvest

"I left school to go to catering college – this was one of the best decisions of my life. Over the next 15 years I worked in food orientated establishments and eventually setting up my own business making jams and chutneys (this after the best decision of my life – having a little girl!). Now a household name throughout Shropshire and further afield, we are assured by customer satisfaction that our chutney is far better than the mass produced alternatives; and we source our ingredients as locally as possible." **Heather Williams**

Carrot and Stilton Stuffed Chicken Breast

1 Heat oven to 200°C (180°C fan). Cut open each chicken breast to create a pocket don't cut completely through.

2 Cut the Stilton into 4 long pieces, put one each into chicken pocket, put 1 heaped tablespoon of Spiced Carrot Chutney into each chicken breast and spread evenly.

3 Lay 4 slices of the Parma ham (or streaky bacon) on a board to form a square. Place the chicken breast on top and wrap tightly round the outside ensuring that the filling is covered. Repeat for the other chicken breasts.

4 Place on an baking tray or oven proof dish and cook for about 20 mins (depending on size of chicken breast) or until completely cooked through.

We like ours with roasted veggies and an extra spoonful of our chutney on the side!

Serves: 4
- 4 chicken breasts
- 4 heaped tablespoons Heather's Harvest Spiced Carrot Chutney
- 160g Stilton
- 16 slices Parma ham (or streaky bacon)

Moor Farm Shop

"Moor Farm was purchased by our family in 1919 and is now a 5th generation business. Our shop grew from a simple meat box scheme which my sister Melissa and I started in 2002, when we returned home to the farm to work. It just grew and grew from there and in 2006 we opened the shop you see today, with the best view to accompany a coffee for miles around. Not only that but our food is super local – our eggs are laid by our own chickens, the meat is from our own Gloucester Old Spot pigs and Hereford cattle, and the breadcrumbs are from our homemade bread made daily by our chef. We also produce almost all our own electricity for the farm and tea room from our own solar panels and we use an air-source heating system for water and heat in the tea rooms in the winter. Sustainable!" **Elaine Timmis**

Moor Farm Shop Scotch Eggs

1 Plunge the eggs into boiling water for 6 mins 45 seconds. When the time is up, take the eggs out and place them into ice water or put into a bowl and run the cold tap onto them. Peel the eggs and set aside

2 Remove the skin from the sausages or remove paper from burger. Flatten the meat out on the palm of your hand, making sure it is of similar thickness.

3 Roll the egg in the flour, then place it in the middle of your meat. Wrap the meat around the egg, pinching to seal. Make sure you do not have any holes; the egg should be fully covered in the meat mix.

4 Whisk two eggs and place your breadcrumbs onto a tray. Cover your eggs in the egg wash then the breadcrumbs, repeat this process twice.

5 Once the eggs are covered in breadcrumbs put them into a deep fat fryer at 180°C for 5 mins until golden brown, then remove. Then pop in the oven at 175°C (155°C fan) for 15 mins.

Other flavour alternatives:
At point 2 – place the meat into a bowl and mix with any of the following flavour suggestions:
- Lemon juice and zest from half a lemon with fresh or dried thyme or sage
- Chilli powder or flakes and/or grated garlic
- Caramelised onion
- Sweet chilli sauce
- Tomato ketchup or brown sauce
(All available from Moor Farm Shop)

Get creative and add anything else you like. If you are unsure of the flavour add a small amount to some sausage meat, cook and taste before making the scotch egg.

For each Scotch Egg you will need:
- 1 Moor Farm Shop Free Range Egg
- 2 eggs for egg wash
- Small amount of plain flour
- Handful of breadcrumbs
- 2 thick Moor Farm Shop Sausages or 145g Sausage Meat (made using Moor Farm Gloucester Old Spot Pork) or 1 thick Moor Farm Hereford Beef Burger

All available from Moor Farm Shop.

free range egg

Coopers Gourmet Sausage Rolls

"My maternal grand-parents lived the good life on a small farm, where they reared animals and grew veg. I helped them from seven years of age, and that's what started my passion for great local produce. Although we have only been in production for five years with our gourmet sausage rolls, we now use over two tonnes of local pork per week. A staple snack, ours are both original, and natural. Once tasted, never forgotten!"
Ivan Watkiss

Coopers Pork, Duck and Marmalade Sausage Roll

1 To ensure the duck is rich in flavour, prepare by taking it out of the fridge to reach room temperature 30 mins before cooking. Ensure the room is cool and the duck is covered when doing so. Preheat your oven to 180°C (160°C fan).

2 Roast the duck for 30 mins (alternatively you can dry fry, grill or barbecue for 3-4 mins on each side). Leave it to cool until you can touch with your finger for 10 seconds. Remove the bones from the duck and cut into 5mm pieces.

3 Mix the duck and pork meat with orange juice and marmalade to ensure it is thoroughly combined.

4 On a floured surface, roll out the pastry into a long rectangular shape and to a thickness of 3mm. It does not matter if you cannot perfect the rectangular shape, just trim the edges to form a rectangle.

5 Place the duck and pork mixture onto the centre of the pastry and form into a sausage shape using your hands. You may want to add water to your hands to help shape the mixture. Once the shape has been formed, brush the edge of the pastry with water. Fold the pastry over the duck and pork filling and firm the pastry around the filling.

6 Brush the sausage roll with the whisked egg and cut into 10cm lengths. Bake the sausage rolls for approx. 50 mins, ensuring they reach a core temperature of 75°C.

Enjoy!

Makes: **12 large sausage rolls**
- 600g puff pastry
- 1.3kg pork sausage meat
- 200g duck breast
- 300ml orange juice
- 150g orange marmalade
- 1 egg, whisked (for glazing)
- Water

Trio of Pork

1. For the belly pork, preheat oven to 180°C (160°C fan). With a sharp knife, slice the skin without cutting into the meat. Drizzle over 2 teaspoons rapeseed oil and massage in white pepper and sea salt. Place skin-side up, on a rack in a roasting tin. Cook in the oven for 1 hour, then baste with the juices. Cook for another hour, basting regularly. Remove and place 1 sliced onion, and 2 sprigs of thyme in the roasting tin under the pork. Brush the mixed honey and cumin over the pork, increase the oven to 200°C (180°C fan). Cook for 30 mins, until golden brown. Peel off the crackling and rest for 5-10 mins before serving.

2. For the braised pork cheek, preheat the oven to 160°C (140°C fan). Gently seal the cheeks in 100ml rapeseed oil, remove and place to one side. Add 1 onion, carrot, celery, leek and a crushed garlic clove to the pan and caramelise. Return pork cheeks and 500ml white wine. Reduce the wine by half. Add 175ml chicken stock, 2 springs thyme, rosemary and 20g brown sugar. Braise in the oven for 2-3 hours.

3. For the faggots, dice the pork shoulder, bacon and livers into a course mince. Dice then sweat 1 onion and 1 crushed garlic clove in a saucepan with a small amount of butter until soft. Allow to cool. Using a mixing bowl combine the breadcrumbs, pepper, all spice, chopped parsley, chopped sage and mace. Add the cooled onion and the meat, mix thoroughly. Divide into 4 parts and shape into balls, wrap each ball in caul fat (or you can use thinned out streaky bacon) and store in fridge. Bake the faggots at 180°C (160°C fan) for 30-40 mins until they are cooked through and nicely browned.

4. For the roasted beetroot, remove the leaves from the beetroots leaving a little stalk. Place the beetroot on tin foil in a roasting tray on . Drizzle a little oil over then sprinkle with 2 sprigs thyme and salt. Bake at 180°C (160°C fan) for 35-40 mins until the beetroots are soft. Leave to cool. Using a knife scrape off the skin and remove the stalk, cut each into 6 wedges.

5. For the fondant potatoes, heat 150g butter over a medium heat in a thick bottomed saucepan. Once the butter is foaming, fry the potatoes until deep golden-brown on one side, about 3-4 mins. Turn and fry for a further 3-4 mins, gently add 50ml white wine and cook out the alcohol. Add 75ml stock, 2 crushed garlic cloves and sprigs of thyme place the pan into the oven and cook at 180°C (160°C fan) for 15-20 mins until soft, then remove from stock.

6. For the swede and honey purée, heat 25g butter and sweat off 1 sliced onion and 1 crushed garlic clove until soft (no colour). Add the swede and continue to sweat for 2-3 mins, sprinkle with flour and stir in for 1 minute. Once the flour has cooked out remove from the heat and add the vegetable stock stirring until the flour has dissolved. Cook on a low heat until swede is soft, remove from heat and add honey before using a hand held blender to purée the swede.

7. For the pickled pear, place the 50g brown sugar, red wine vinegar, lemon juice, ginger and 2 cloves garlic in a small saucepan with 100ml water, bring to a boil. Reduce heat and simmer for 5 mins to develop flavours. Add the pears and simmer for a further 5 mins. Remove from heat and place to one side to allow the liquid to permeate the pear. Slice into quarters.

While the belly pork is resting, heat the juices in the roasting tray, adding 100ml white wine and 100ml chicken stock and reduce by half. Strain and serve over all completed elements arranged on the plates.

Serves: 4

- 800g pork belly (skin on, bones removed)
- Rapeseed oil
- 4 medium onions
- 1 bunch of thyme
- 2-3 teaspoons honey
- ½ teaspoon ground cumin
- 650ml white wine
- 1.2 litres chicken stock
- 4 pork cheeks
- 1 carrot
- 1 celery stick
- 1 leek
- 7 garlic cloves
- 2 sprigs of rosemary
- 70g brown sugar
- 150g pigs livers, soaked in milk
- 150g Maynard's pork shoulder
- 100g Maynard's smoked bacon
- 90g breadcrumbs
- Chopped fresh parsley
- Chopped fresh sage
- 1 small egg
- 150g caul fat, soaked in cold water
- A pinch of mace, pepper and all spice
- 2 fresh beetroots, washed under cold running water and dried
- 175g butter
- 4 potatoes, peeled, cut into barrels
- 2-3 sprigs of fresh thyme
- 350g swede, peeled and diced
- 25g flour
- 250ml vegetable stock
- 100ml honey
- 2 conference pears
- 250ml red wine vinegar
- 1 lemon, juiced
- 2cm fresh ginger, peeled and diced

Shrewsbury College

"Courses in hospitality and catering at Shrewsbury College have led our students into successful careers all over the country. The roots of the college can be traced back to 1899. Many students educated here have become world famous, including Wilfred Owen the noted war poet. An interesting fact that you probably didn't know and has no relevance to catering but you heard it from us! Shropshire is home to the worlds first skyscraper, Ditherington Flax Mill. Built in 1797, it's the world's first multi-story iron framed building, a technique still used today for skyscrapers!" **Dan Gibbons**

thyme

Buttercross Farm

"Developing our artisan pork, ham and bacon business has been a therapeutic response to the terrible income that we endured when we were supplying pigs to large scale retailers via wholesalers and pig industry marketeers. Having created our own brand we now sell in Shropshire, the Midlands and even throughout the whole of Europe. Our sausages are special – we make enough sausages every year that if laid end to end they would stretch from Market Drayton to Oswestry – about 40 miles. That's a lot of sausage!" **Martyn Rowley**

Individual Buttercross Toad in Hole

Served with Caramelised Shallots and Thyme Gravy

1 Mix the batter ingredients together, whisk constantly for 10-15 mins with an electric whisk. Sieve out any lumps, season and rest in the fridge for 20 mins. Preheat oven to 200°C (180°C fan).

2 Pan fry, then roast sausages in the oven for 10 mins in their individual tins. This allows the tins to get nice and hot before adding the batter. Pour over the batter, and bake for 15-20 mins until the batter has risen and is golden.

3 Fry off the shallots gently in the butter, oil and honey, then roast in the oven until golden brown, season.

4 For the gravy, fry the vegetables and herbs in oil, until golden. Add tomato purée, fry off for another 2-3 mins. Add red wine and reduce by half. Add stock and thyme, reduce until thick. Remove any fat from the surface, sieve, then finish with a few fresh thyme leaves.

Serve in their individual tins, drizzled with the gravy.

Serves: 4
- 12 thin or 8 thick Buttercross Farm Sausages

For the batter:
- 160g flour
- 200ml milk
- 2 duck eggs whole
- 1 egg yolk

For the shallots:
- 200g shallots, peeled and sliced
- 40g butter
- Drizzle of oil
- 2 tablespoons local honey

For the gravy:
- 250ml chicken stock
- 200ml red wine
- 1 carrot
- 2 celery sticks
- 1 large onion
- 2 garlic cloves, crushed
- 1 bay leaf
- 3 sprigs of thyme
- 1 tablespoon tomato purée

Willo Game

"All our game is sourced from the wild, the great thing about this is that it couldn't be more natural and free-range. Being able to roam and eat as they please gives our venison and game birds a varied diet and so a depth and richness of flavour not found in commercially farmed meat. The other wonderful thing about wild game is that it is naturally low in fat and venison in particular is high in iron so it is also a healthy option. Due to the low fat levels it is important not to overcook game otherwise it will dry out, but cooked correctly it is tender and succulent" **Ben Bowyer**

Pan Roast Loin of Venison

Served with Creamed Celeriac, Celeriac Gratin, Ruby Chard and a 'Shropshire Prune' Damson Sauce

1 For the damson sauce, fry off venison trim and bones in the oil until brown, add onions, garlic, celery, carrot, thyme, bay and peppercorns. Fry off gently. Add the damson vinegar and red wine, reduce by half. Add the water (or stock) reduce by half again. Skim off any fat and sieve, add the damsons cook out for 10-15 mins or until thick and syrupy. Taste and season.

2 For the creamed celeriac, gently cook the celeriac in the milk on a low heat, until tender. Blend until smooth. Add butter and continue blending. Pass through fine sieve and season.

3 For the celeriac gratin, preheat the oven to 190°C (170°C fan). Bring the cream, milk, garlic, and rosemary to the boil, season liberally, simmer for 10 mins then sieve. Grease a deep roasting tin, finely slice the celeriac 2mm thick, layer with flavoured cream, bake for 40-50 mins, until the celeriac's tender and the top is browned and crisp.

4 For the venison, heat an ovenproof frying pan with oil, add the venison loin, season on all sides, cook until brown on all sides, usually 1 or 2 mins. Place in a preheated oven at 200°C (180°C fan), cook for 6-8 mins, turn occasionally. Remove from oven add butter, thyme, garlic to the pan. Rest for 10 mins, basting with the butter. Remove venison from the pan and slice. Add chard leaves into the warm butter, to lightly wilt.

To finish, plate the creamed celeriac, a slice of the gratin, the chard then venison and drizzle over the sauce.

Serves: 6

For the damson sauce:
- 50ml rapeseed oil
- 450g venison trim, bones, chopped small from the saddle
- 1 onion, chopped
- 2 garlic cloves, crushed
- 1 celery stick, chopped
- 1 carrot, chopped
- 1 thyme sprig
- 1 bay leaf
- 6 peppercorns
- 40ml damson vinegar (Chilton or other)
- 400ml red wine
- 1 litre water or chicken or veal stock
- 30-40 damsons (Shropshire Prune variety)

For the creamed celeriac:
- 250g celeriac, peeled and cubed
- 225ml milk
- 70g butter

For the celeriac gratin:
- 10ml rapeseed oil
- 1kg celeriac, peeled
- 1 large sprig rosemary, leaves finely chopped
- 4 garlic cloves
- Salt and black pepper
- 400ml double cream
- 100ml milk

For the venison loin:
- 6 Willo Game Venison Loin Steak approx. 200g (or more if you like)
- 35ml rapeseed oil
- 50g butter
- 1 thyme sprig
- 1 garlic clove
- 15-20 ruby chard leaves (or beetroot tops)

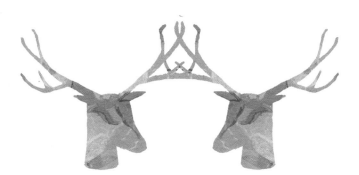

Ludlow Brewing Company

"A converted railway shed houses our brewery. Originally constructed in the 1850's and now fully refurbished and housing a 20 barrel brewing system. As well as producing award winning high quality ales, we also ensure that we have an environmentally friendly business – heat reclaimed during the brewing process is used for underfloor heating, we recycle rainwater, have low carbon insulation, use low energy lighting and have installed solar panels. Our hops don't come far either – just trundled up the road from Tenbury Wells. Did you know that there is a word for the 'fear of an empty beer glass' – cenosillicaphobia. No fear of that around here!" **Gary and Alison Walters**

Black Knight Treacle Glazed Ham

1 Drain the gammon and place in a large saucepan. Immerse the joint fully in cold water, then slowly bring to the boil. With a large metal spoon skim off any froth and scum that rises to the surface. Simmer for a few minutes, then carefully pour off the water from the pot, along with any more froth and scum.

2 Add the onion, carrot, leek, cinnamon stick, bay leaves and peppercorns to the gammon in the pot and pour in the stout. Top with enough cold water to ensure the ham is completely covered. Bring to a simmer and cook partially covered for 2½ hours over a gentle heat. Skim off any scum that surfaces during cooking and top up with boiling water as necessary.

3 Remove the ham from the pot and rest on a board. Preheat the oven to 190°C (170°C fan). Peel off the skin, leaving behind an even layer of fat, about 5mm thick. Use a sharp knife to score the fat in a crisscross pattern at 1.5cm intervals. Stud each diamond with a clove. Transfer the ham to a medium roasting tray.

4 Mix together all the ingredients for the glaze and brush half of it over the ham. Roast for 15 mins, then pour over the rest of the glaze and continue to roast for a further 10-15 mins, basting every 5 mins. Remove from the oven and give the ham a final basting with the pan juices. Leave to rest before carving into thin slices.

We love our ham as a Boxing Day treat.

Once you have roasted your ham, it will keep in the fridge for two days and is delicious served cold too.

Serves: 8
- 2kg unsmoked, boneless gammon joint, soaked overnight
- large onion, peeled and roughly chopped
- large carrot, peeled and roughly chopped
- large leek, trimmed and roughly chopped
- large cinnamon stick
- 2 bay leaves
- 1 teaspoon black peppercorns
- 2 x 500ml bottles Black Knight Stout
- Cloves, to stud

For the glaze:
- 60ml treacle
- 2 tablespoons Dijon mustard
- 1 tablespoon soy sauce
- 1 tablespoon Worcestershire sauce
- 60g light soft brown sugar

Pig...

Shropshire Lamb Three Ways

Michel Nijsten's Slow Roast Shoulder, Grilled Lamb Cutlet and Lamb Faggot served with Baby Vegetables, Pea Purée and Purple Potatoes

1 For the slow roast shoulder, glaze the shallot and garlic on low heat in a little olive oil, then add chopped rosemary and leave to cool. Place the shoulder, skin side down onto a chopping board, remove any visible fat lumps with a sharp knife. Season the lamb with salt and black pepper and spread the shallot mixture onto the meat evenly. Roll the shoulder into a tight roulade-type shape and tie with string starting in the middle, then on the outsides and two more times between the middle to each outer side.

2 Heat a roasting tin, big enough to nestle the shoulder in, add a little oil, then brown the outside of the lamb. Add the diced vegetables and bones then sit the lamb on top. Deglaze with cooking wine and add a little stock, cover the meat with greaseproof paper then cover with foil, so all is sealed tight inside the tin. Slow roast in the oven at 125°C (105°C fan) for 3-4 hours. The shoulder will be perfect when, if pierced with a skewer the skewer can be pulled out without any resistance. Leave to cool for 24 hours

3 For the faggots, preheat the oven to 170°C (150°C fan). Mix the lamb breast, heart, liver and pork belly together until well combined. Add the parsley and thyme. Heat a pan over a low-medium heat, add oil, the shallot and garlic and leave to sweat down. Once soft, but not coloured, deglaze with the port and cook until reduced to a syrup. Add to the faggot mix. Add a liberal amount of salt and pepper, the egg and oats. Make a very small patty out of the mix and cook in a frying pan. Check the seasoning, adding more salt and pepper if needed. Roll the faggots into 12 evenly sized balls and set aside while you prepare the caul fat.

4 Rinse the caul fat in cold water and lay out on a board. Place a rolled faggot in the centre of the caul fat, wrap until totally sealed then cut away with a knife. Shape into a nice ball then repeat to make 12 faggots. Heat some oil in a frying pan over a low-medium heat. Once hot, colour each side of the faggots, ensuring the pan is not too hot – as this may cause them to split. Set aside in the fridge for at least 10 mins.

5 For the cutlets, griddle to mark the cutlets crossing marks, then heat until pink. Pass the shoulder stock through a fine sieve and reduce to form a jus. Slice the shoulder into 1.5cm round disks and put onto a baking sheet lined with greaseproof paper, place cutlets and faggots alongside. Place on cleaned and cooked baby turnips, baby carrots and diced purple potatoes, place knobs of butter on the vegetables and cover with greaseproof paper. Put into a preheated oven of 150°C (130°C fan) for 8-10 mins until centre of the shoulder is hot and cutlets are pink.

6 Place a dollop of hot pea purée on the plate, spread the purée in one stroke. Place on the shoulder to one side, then set the cutlet and faggot onto it. Place cooked baby vegetables with cooked and cubed purple potatoes around the meats. Drizzle the faggot with little jus. Enjoy.

Serves: 4

For the slow roast shoulder:
- 800g boneless shoulder of lamb (bones for stock)
- 1 banana shallot, peeled and finely diced
- 2 cloves garlic, diced
- 1 sprig rosemary leaves, chopped
- 1 medium carrot, diced
- 1 celery stick, diced
- 1 red onion, diced
- 1 leek, sliced
- Splash of cooking wine
- A little stock

For the lamb cutlets:
- 4 decent size French trimmed cutlets
- Rosemary, chopped

For the lamb faggot:
- 100g lamb breast, minced
- 80g lamb heart, minced
- 80g lamb liver, minced
- 80g pork belly, minced
- 25g of caul fat
- 5g flat leaf parsley, chopped
- 6 sprigs of fresh thyme, stripped
- 1 banana shallot, diced
- 1 garlic clove, finely diced
- 1 egg
- 20g oats
- A dash of port

Also:
- Sea salt and black pepper
- Olive oil
- Baby vegetables
- Pea purée
- Purple potatoes

Albright Hussey Manor Hotel

"Although we have only been running our hotel for 27 years the history of our building goes back to the 13th century. First recorded in the Domesday Book as "Elbretone", today The Albright Hussey retains all the charm and character of its history. In 1292, to avoid confusion with other place names similar to "Albrighton" the name "Hussey" was added after the family who occupied it, not after a woman of loose virtue! The present house, was rebuilt in 1524 with mainly timber frame, and moated for protection. We are Italian, our chef is Dutch but our roots are now Shropshire and we use as much local produce in our menus as we can." **Paul Subbiani**

The Foundry

"Our Shrewsbury Theatre restaurant will very much form a memorable part of your thespian evening. The meal will punctuate the performance with the table dedicated to your party so that you can come back and eat your desserts and sip your drinks during the interval. Built on the site of an old foundry beside the river Severn this is a fabulous site for my first solo venture after 18 years in the catering trade. Let the action begin!" **Matthew Periam**

Thyme Roasted Corn Fed Chicken Supreme

Served with Fondant Potato, Creamed Savoy Cabbage, Roast Shallot and Red Wine Jus

1 Let's start by making that really yummy gravy. Heat a heavy based saucepan over a high heat and add the cooking oil, shallot, garlic and thyme. Frequently stir until the shallots have softened and gone a nice golden brown colour. Don't worry if the pan is a bit brown as that is full of flavour! Next, pour half the bottle of the red wine into the pan (pour yourself a glass with the other half and enjoy while you cook!), get a wooden spoon and give a good hard stir, scraping the brown bits from the bottom of the pan, this is known as deglazing. Add the bay leaf, reduce the liquid until it is a third of its original volume. Add the chicken stock and again reduce the liquid by half, to concentrate the flavour. Strain the liquid through a sieve into another pan reserving the liquid. Mix the cornflour with a tablespoon of water and add to the gravy stirring well, if the gravy is not thick enough to your liking, repeat this corn flour process until your desired result. Leave to one side.

2 If you are feeling confident you can get the fondant potatoes ready while you wait for the wine to reduce. Peel the potatoes and trim into barrel shapes, better still use a cutter to create a neat circle. Heat the oil in a wide based pan on a high heat and add the potatoes. You want to get a small amount of colour but be careful that they do not stick. Once you have achieved a small amount of colour add the butter. Leave the potatoes on a high heat and check every 5 mins until the potatoes are soft through the middle when pierced with a knife. If the butter stops frothing you run the risk of burning the butter. If this happens carefully remove the potatoes from the pan and place on a baking tray, you can now roast the potatoes until they are soft through the middle.

3 Grab a frying pan big enough to fit the 4 chicken breasts, add the cooking oil and put on a high heat. Season the chicken breasts with salt and pepper Place into the hot pan, skin side down (be careful as they may spit). Once you achieve a nice golden brown colour, flip the chicken breasts over, add the knob of butter and thyme and place in the oven at 180°C (160°C fan).

4 For the shallots, add the cooking oil to a baking tray and heat in the oven. Meanwhile peel the shallots and slice them in half lengthways. Place the shallots face down in icing sugar making sure they have a nice thin layer covering them. Take the baking tray out of the oven and place the shallots face down, put straight back in the oven and roast for 5 mins, or until they're soft and golden.

5 Now it's time to get the cabbage working. Here is the time to multi task! Finely chop the cabbage into strips and add to a pan of boiling salted water. Meanwhile pop the garlic and double cream into another pan. Bring the cream to boil and then lower the heat to minimum. You want to reduce the cream to achieve a thick 'coat the back of a spoon' consistency. While the cream is reducing, heat another pan on a high heat, add a tablespoon of cooking oil along with the bacon lardons. Ensure you stir frequently and cook the lardons until they are nice and crispy. As soon as the lardons are cooking it should be time to drain the cabbage. You want the cabbage to still have a bite to it. Add the drained cabbage back to a pan, add the crispy lardons and the reduced cream and stir all together. Drain any excess cream.

6 Finally, peel the baby carrots and boil them in a pan with the orange juice and sugar until the carrots are just soft.

All that's left to do is to make sure everything is hot and present them together in a way that suits your creative flair!

Serves: 4

For the chicken:
- 4 free range corn fed chicken breasts
- 2 sprigs of thyme
- 1 knob of butter
- 1 tablespoon of cooking oil

For the red wine jus (really yummy gravy!):
- 1 bottle of your favourite red wine
- 570ml chicken stock (nothing beats home made)
- 1 banana shallot, roughly chopped
- 2 garlic cloves, minced or grated
- 2 sprigs of thyme
- 1 bay leaf
- 1 tablespoon cooking oil
- 1 tablespoon cornflour

For the fondant potato:
- 4 baking potatoes
- 250g salted butter
- 1 tablespoon cooking oil

For the sweet roasted shallot:
- 2 banana shallots
- 1 tablespoon cooking oil
- 100g icing sugar

For the creamed cabbage:
- 1 savoy cabbage
- 200g smoked bacon lardons
- 1 garlic clove, minced or grated
- 200ml double cream

For the garnish:
- 16 baby carrots
- 240ml orange juice
- 1 tablespoon caster sugar

Harper Adams

"The food sector plays a huge role in contributing to the UK's economy and the health, welfare and sustainability of the population and the environment. Established in 1901, Harper Adams University is a key link in this chain supporting not only education but vital research in the agri-food industry. Our catering services places special attention on the ethical sourcing of our food, promoting local sourcing and sustainability through our courses and through our own practice. We also source from our own campus farm including beef, pork, lamb and eggs. We produce 16 miles of sausages every year, if laid out, they would nearly stretch to Shrewsbury!" **Maxine Hughes**

Fillet of Harper Beef

Served with a Café de Paris Butter, Chunky Chips and Vine Roasted Cherry Tomatoes

1 Mix all of the ingredients for the butter together in a bowl, beat with a wooden spoon until all ingredients are incorporated into the butter. The butter should be bright yellow in colour. Form the butter into a thick cylinder shape, wrap in cling film and pop into the fridge to set. Tip – extra butter can be frozen for later use.

2 For the chunky chips, cut the potatoes into large even sized rectangles and place into a deep fat fryer at 140°C until soft. Store chips in the fridge until chilled. When chips are required, cook at 180°C until golden brown. Drain onto kitchen paper and season with salt.

3 Place the cherry tomatoes on the vine into an oven proof dish, add the demerara sugar and balsamic vinegar and roast until they start to wrinkle.

4 Cook the fillet steaks to your liking. Slice the butter and place on top of the steak, add the chips and cherry tomatoes, and enjoy!

Serves: 4
- 4 fillets quality beef
- 300g cherry tomatoes, on the vine
- 1 teaspoon demerara sugar
- 1 teaspoon balsamic vinegar
- 4 large potatoes, peeled
- Oil, for deep frying

For the Café de Paris butter:
- 250g salted butter, softened
- 1 teaspoon pernod
- 1 teaspoon brandy
- 1 teaspoon Worcester sauce
- 2 teaspoons curry powder
- 2 cloves of garlic, crushed
- 1 small bunch parsley, chopped
- ½ teaspoon cumin
- ½ teaspoon turmeric
- ½ teaspoon lemon juice
- 1 tablespoon tomato ketchup

Shrewsbury Food Festival

"Having helped organise Ludlow Food Festival for many years, I have seen the opportunities and economic benefits these events bring to the town, producers and community. Shrewsbury's exceptional food scene has been a well kept secret for too long and so our festival brings Shrewsbury's (and Shropshire's) epicurean delights to the forefront. This year we had 23000 visitors and over 200 producers at our family friendly festival with tons of free entertainment and foodie activities. The festival was born from a passion for great food, fantastic producers and a love for our stunning landscape. We are proud to be a small part of the magnificent Shropshire food family!" **Beth Heath**

Roast Haunch of Wild Boar

Served with Sage and Honey, Chestnut Mushrooms, Hassleback Potatoes and Heritage Carrots

1 You should marinate your boar for at least 2 hours (up to 8 hours) before cooking. Massage the meat with the garlic, honey, mustard, salt and pepper. Pop into a food bag, and add the orange juice, oil, vinegar, sage, rosemary and thyme. Seal the bag well, and pop into the fridge.

2 Once marinated, line a roasting tin with parchment paper. Place the boar on top, scatter round the chopped onion and tomatoes, then pour over the rest of the marinade, and dot with a little butter. Cover with the parchment and then cover the tin tightly with 2 layers of foil. Cook for 10 mins at 230°C (210°C fan) then reduce the oven temp to 180°C (160°C fan) 45 mins per kilo (so our 750g haunch was cooked for 34 mins).

3 Cut into the potatoes thin slices across almost right through, but not quite. A wooden spoon will help. Pop each potato into the spoon and slice down The curve of the spoon will help you not cut through the potato. Pop them into a baking tin with the oil and butter and heat on the hob, basting with the fat. Sprinkle with salt and transfer to the oven for 40 mins.

4 Remove the foil and top parchment from the boar and cook for 10 mins longer to allow the top to get a lovely colour.

5 Pop the carrots into a saucepan with the butter, sugar and salt. Pour in water to cover the carrots halfway, bring to the boil. Reduce to a simmer and cook for 15-20 mins until tender. Turn up the heat to cook until the water has evaporated leaving a buttery glaze. Toss in the thyme leaves.

6 For the mushrooms, heat a heavy frying pan with the oil and butter, pop in the mushrooms and toss to coat. Cook over a medium heat until the mushrooms start to soften. Tip – avoid stirring too much as this releases the water out the mushrooms, causing them to steam rather than fry. Add the crushed garlic about half way through, and cook until garlic is golden and fragrant. Add wine and cook until evaporated. Finish with the rosemary.

7 While the boar is resting, quickly make a sauce with the roasting juices. Add the Applejack to the tin and flambé, stir to remove any sticky bits off the edges (these have the best flavour!), cook to reduce if necessary. Pass through a sieve, and serve over the meat.

Serves: 4
- 750g Willo Game Wild Boar Haunch, boned and rolled
- 2 cloves garlic, crushed
- 3 tablespoons Shropshire honey
- 1 tablespoon mild mustard
- 1 orange, juiced
- 70ml Bennett and Dunn Rapeseed Oil
- 1 tablespoon wine vinegar
- 1 sprig sage leaves, chopped
- 1 sprig rosemary
- 1 sprig thyme, leaves picked
- 2 tomatoes, roughly chopped
- 1 onion, roughly chopped
- 1 small knob butter
- 60ml Ludlow Distillery Applejack
- Salt and freshly milled pepper

For the hassleback potatoes:
- 12 local potatoes, oval shaped
- 40g butter
- 3 tablespoons Bennett and Dunn Rapeseed Oil

For the carrots:
- 500g heritage carrots
- 15g butter
- 2 teaspoons caster sugar
- 1 sprig thyme leaves, lightly chopped

For the mushrooms:
- 400g chestnut mushrooms
- 1 clove garlic, crushed
- 1 tablespoons Bennett and Dunn Rapeseed Oil
- 1 tablespoon butter
- 70ml dry white wine
- 1 sprig rosemary, finely chopped

Treflach Farm

"Our family farm and Community Interest Company provides education about farming, food production and the environment and we have managed to help to fund this through the sale of tasty home made pies. In the family for 110 years and 4 generations, our vision for the farm and for agriculture is rooted in the community. A sustainable industry working in harmony with nature and providing for the needs of local people. Our produce is at the heart of this philosophy linking people, animal welfare in food production, sustainability and care for the environment. Even our pies are wholesome too!" **Ian Steele**

Serves: 4-6

- 1kg diced beef
- 300ml Stonehouse Brewery Off the Rails Ale
- 1 onion, diced
- 1 tablespoon veg oil
- 150ml beef stock
- Salt, pepper and herbs, to taste
- 175g Shropshire Blue cheese, in chunks

For the suet crust:

- 225g self raising flour
- A pinch of salt
- 100g shredded suet
- 100g grated Shropshire Red cheese
- 2 tablespoons chopped parsley

Beef and Blue Pie with Suet Crust

1 Gently fry the diced onion in the oil until soft, then add the beef and stir until coated. Add the ale, stock, salt, pepper and herbs, stir well. Simmer on a medium heat until beef is tender, 1-2 hours. Pour into pie dish, and top with chunks of Shropshire Blue cheese.

2 Meanwhile, mix flour, salt, suet, grated cheese and chopped parsley. Add sufficient cold water to mix to a pliable dough. Roll out the dough to approx. 2cm thick (thicker will be more dumpling-like, thinner will be more crispy, 2cm is about right to make it dumpling-like underneath and crispy on top).

3 Cover the beef mixture with the dough, and bake at 180°C (160°C fan) for about 30 mins until the pie is golden brown.

Beef Cow

The Wood Brewery

sage

"Our brewing commenced in April 1980 and is still in the hands of the founding family. Our 'Shropshire Lad' was originally brewed to commemorate the centenary of the publication of A E Houseman's collection of poems of the same name.

Leave your home behind, lad,
And reach your friends your hand,
And go, and luck go with you,
While Ludlow tower shall stand.

Travelling south to the Boer War he should have also been fortified by one of our 30 million pints brewed so far." **Edward Wood**

Shropshire Lad Ale Braised Pork Chop

Served with Ale, Mustard Cream Sauce, Savoy Cabbage and Honey Roast Parsnips

1 For the chops, fry off the onion and garlic in the oil and butter until a light golden colour, add the Shropshire Lad Ale, sage and thyme, reduce by two thirds. Add the chicken stock.

2 In a separate pan, fry off chops on both sides until brown, season. Place in the reduced ale/stock mix in an ovenproof pan or dish. Cook in preheated oven at 150°C (130°C fan) for 1-1.5 hours, until cooked.

3 For the parsnips, poach the parsnips in simmering water for 10 mins until par cooked, remove and drain. Then fry in butter and oil until golden, drizzle over honey and thyme leaves. Bake for 10-20 mins in oven at 200°C (180°C fan).

4 For the Savoy cabbage, bring butter and water to boil, add leaves, cook for 5 mins or until soft, season.

5 Once the pork is cooked remove it carefully from stock, rest under foil while you finish the sauce. Reduce cooking liquor down until thick, add the cream, milk, honey and mustard, bring to the simmer. Sieve and season to taste if needed.

To plate, mix the parsnips and cabbage and arrange onto plate, place cooked chop on top and drizzle over the sauce.

Serves: 2

For the chops:
- 2 onions white, finely diced
- 3 cloves of garlic, finely diced
- 1 knob of butter
- 1 drizzle of oil
- 250ml Shropshire Lad Ale
- 1 sprig of thyme
- 3 sage leaves
- 300ml chicken stock
- 2 rare breed pork chops (Gloucester Old Spot, Tamworth or Middlewhite)
- 200ml double cream
- 150ml milk
- 1 tablespoon honey
- 1 tablespoon wholegrain mustard
- Salt and pepper

For the parsnips:
- 2-3 large parsnips, peeled and sliced into chip sized pieces (remove core if woody)
- 30g butter
- 1 drizzle of hazelnut oil
- 1 sprig of thyme
- 1 drizzle of local honey

For the Savoy cabbage:
- 50g butter
- 100ml water
- 6-8 savoy cabbage leaves, stems removed and chopped into squares

Rabbit with Acorns and Chestnuts

1 Beer vinegar must be made 3 weeks in advance. Put the beer into a container with red wine vinegar. Cover with cling film and leave for 3 weeks. After the 3 weeks, put container into freezer. Once frozen, put the frozen beer vinegar into a sieve or colander lined with J-cloth and leave to defrost into a different container. Once passed it is now ready to be used. Beer vinegar can be stored in an airtight container indefinitely.

2 For the chestnut sand, blitz chestnuts in food processor. Heat a frying pan, add rapeseed oil, chestnuts and a pinch of salt. Fry until crispy. Heat oven to lowest possible temperature. Put crispy chestnuts into a tray and into the oven for two hours until they have dried out. Once dry, blitz in food processor until it becomes a powder, pass powder through sieve.

3 To make the clover oil, put the clover and oil into sous vide bag, seal. Set waterbath to 90°C, add bag with clover and oil and leave for 1 hour. Take the bag out of waterbath and leave to cool naturally. Take the liquid out of bag and blitz until smooth. Pass through a sieve lined with a J-cloth. All that should be left is a green tinted oil.

4 To make the chestnut tuille, mix chestnut purée and sugar, whisk together. Add melted butter, whisk. Add flour, whisk until all incorporated. Leave to rest in fridge for one hour. Set oven to 180°C (160°C fan). Using offset handle spatula, spread smooth layer of tuille mix into a rectangle stencil on a non-stick mat. Remove stencil and cook in oven for 10 mins until golden brown. Take out of oven and leave to cool for 45 seconds. Using spatula, work tuille off non-stick mat and roll around a suitably sized cylinder, I used a whisk handle. Leave to cool and harden and then very gently slide off handle.

5 For the acorn pannacotta, bring milk and cream to a boil then take off the heat, add acorn flavour until you reach required taste and add pinch of salt. Bloom gelatine in cold water, when soft, squeeze out excess water and add to the milk/cream mixture. Blitz with an immersion blender. Strain through a sieve into a piping bag, leave to set in piping bag. Once set, pipe the soft pannacotta into the tuille.

6 For the beer vinegar fluid gel, put 500ml of your beer vinegar into a pan with the agar agar, heat until just below boiling point, cook for 20 seconds longer then take off heat. Leave to set in fridge. Once set, put into blender and blend on high speed for 10 mins. Pass through sieve into squeezy bottle.

7 For the hay foam, place hay into a sous vide bag with 500ml of water and seal. Put in a waterbath set at 90°C for 1 hour. Take out and strain through a sieve. Add soy lecithin in a ratio of 0.5% of total weight of hay consommé i.e 2.5g per 500ml. Blitz with hand blender to get "hay foam" scoop foam off with spoon and add to final dish.

8 For the rabbit, trim the loin from the rabbit. Lay a length of cling film on a surface approx. 60cm long, use a cloth to wipe and make sure there are no bubbles. Repeat this so that there are two layers of cling film covering each other. Put the loin in the middle of the cling film next to the edge closest to you and roll tightly to a cigar shape, tie one end of the cling film and then keep rolling until the meat is tight within the cling film, tie the other side of cling film. You should now have a sausage shape rabbit loin surrounded in cling film.

9 Seal the rabbit in sous vide bag. Cook in a waterbath set at 58°C for 45 mins. Take meat out of waterbath, strip away cling film and brown in a hot pan with rapeseed oil and butter. At this point season generously with Maldon Sea Salt.

Assemble carefully all the elements on the plate.

Serves: **4-8**

For the beer vinegar:
- 2 pints of ale (I used Salopian breweries, Shropshire Gold)
- 2 tablespoons red wine vinegar

For the chestnut sand:
- 50g ready to use chestnuts
- Pinch of salt
- Rapeseed oil

For the clover oil:
- 100g freshly picked clover
- 100g rapeseed oil

For the chestnut tuille:
- 100g chestnut purée
- 200g caster sugar
- 90g chestnut flour
- 100g unsalted butter

For the acorn pannacotta:
- 500g full fat milk
- 500g double cream
- Acorn flavour drops
- Pinch of Maldon Sea Salt
- 7 sheets gelatine

For the beer vinegar fluid gel:
- 500ml beer vinegar
- 6g agar agar

For the hay foam:
- 25g hay
- 500ml water
- Soy lecithin

- 1 rabbit loin per person
- Maldon Sea Salt
- Rapeseed oil
- Generous knob of butter

Henry Tudor House

"The inspiration to our young business is working in our iconic building. Vibrant and relevant to Shrewsbury's economy and culture, Henry Tudor House was already 50 years old when Henry Tudor (aka Henry VII) sought refuge here on his way to the Battle of Bosworth, where his army killed King Richard III ending the Plantagenet dynasty and claiming the throne for the Tudors. In fact he was crowned on the battlefield. Intrinsically British, our music, cuisine, art and atmosphere is aided and abetted by our historic building." **James Sherwin**

Netherton Foundry

"Our Foundry is a family owned business located in South Shropshire producing an eco sustainable product made from natural and locally sourced oak, iron and flax oil. We sit right in the birthplace of the European Industrial Revolution. This was the 18th Century's "Silicon Valley". Today the heavy iron and coal industries are all but a distant memory and, for the most part, this corner of rural England has returned to a much quieter way of life. Here at the Foundry we are inspired by the 18th and 19th centuries' Shropshire Iron masters, especially Abraham Darby, creator of the world's first iron bridge. We love the values that inspired this amazing period of creativity and energy but we hope to learn from their mistakes and avoid the misuse of our beautiful county." **Neil Currie**

Shrewsbury Sausages

Sausages and beans slowly cooked together to produce a rich dish perfect for sharing on a cold winter's evening.

1 Place the cast iron bowl on the hob over a medium heat. Heat the oil in the cast iron bowl and brown the sausages on all sides. Place the browned sausages on a plate and reserve.

2 Place the onion and garlic into the cast iron bowl and sauté on the hob, until softened.

3 Carefully transfer the bowl to the heater base and add the rest of the ingredients. Return the sausages to the bowl and cover with the lid. Cook on LOW for 4-6 hours, relax!

Serve with crusty bread and a cold beer.

Serves: 6-8
- 2 tablespoons sunflower oil
- 12-16 good quality local sausages (we love Middle Farm sausages)
- 4 onions, chopped
- 4 garlic cloves, chopped
- 4 carrots, chopped
- 4 bay leaves
- 2 tablespoons fresh thyme leaves
- 200ml red wine
- 4 tablespoons tomato purée
- 100ml stock
- 2 x 400g tin tomatoes
- 4 x 400g butter beans

The Pheasant at Neenton

"A community pub is something of a tautology! All pubs are communities, gathering places and this social enterprise has been very successful in meeting its objectives. The Pheasant is one of 600 pubs in England registered as an Asset of Community Value and one of around 30 co-operative owned pubs in the UK. The benefit of the community owning a pub is that everyone engages to make it something better, more special and a great place to meet and eat. We've a great Shropshire menu using local ingredients and suppliers, real ales and interesting wines and stylish bedrooms for visitors and diners to stay over." **Mark Harris**

Smoked Cod Loin

Served with Wild Garlic, New Potatoes and White Wine Cream

1 For the garlic oil, blend the garlic, and oil in a food processor then warm the mixture in a pan until 100°C, chill over ice then strain through a coffee filter and set aside.

2 For the white wine cream, boil the wine in a pan until it has reduced by half, then add the stock and reduce the mixture by half, then add the cream and continue to reduce until a good consistency is created.

3 Preheat the oven to 180°C (160°C fan). Slice the new potatoes in half-length ways, drizzle with oil and season with salt and pepper then bake in the oven for 20-25 mins.

4 Pat dry the cod skin, season with the salt and pepper, warm a non-stick frying pan over a medium heat then add a drizzle of oil and place the cod skin side down carefully into the pan. Cook the cod for 4-5 mins until the skin is lightly browned and crispy. Turn the fish, cook for a further 3 mins then add half the diced butter to the pan and pull aside to rest.

5 Warm a medium pan over a medium heat then add the rest of the butter, once melted add the leeks and cook without colouring, once cooked add the white wine cream then the wild garlic and fold through the mixture.

6 Place the cherry tomatoes in a tray and drizzle with oil and season with salt and pepper then bake for 5-6 mins or until the skin cracks.

Build the dish however best suits your style.

Serves: **4**
- 4 x 200g smoked cod loin
- 20 cherry tomatoes
- 16 new potatoes
- 350g leeks, washed and finely sliced
- 120g wild garlic, washed
- 125g diced butter
- 200ml rapeseed oil
- Salt and pepper

For the wild garlic oil:
- 100g wild garlic
- 325ml rapeseed oil

For the white wine cream:
- 100ml white wine
- 100ml fish (or vegetable) stock
- 100ml double cream

Ironbridge Catering

"We set up our catering company using a redundancy package. What a great opportunity that was – we have since gone from strength to strength providing the catering backdrop to events county-wide. Our 15-foot mobile BBQ smoker is one of the largest mobile BBQs in the country. We only use local meats (and local hardwoods for the fire) creating a deliciously individual flavour. Etymologists believe that barbecue derives from the word barabicu found in the language of the Taíno people of Caribbean – we have our own roots here in Shropshire!" **Kevin Guerin**

Bloody Mary Beef Brisket

1 In a large oven proof dish, place the brisket and season with salt and pepper on both sides. Combine the rest of the ingredients and pour over the beef.

2 Place a sheet of greaseproof paper on top (this protects the meat from burning and sticking to the tinfoil) and cover with tinfoil to trap in the steam. Cook on a low heat – 120°C (100°C fan) for up to 12 hours.

3 Take it out of the oven and let it rest for ½ hour. Carefully take the covers off the pan and pour the meat juices for now into a jug.

4 Using 2 forks, the meat can be separated into strips. I make cuts across the cooked joint every 6-8 inches beforehand to make serving it easier. Once the meat is separated most, if not all the juice can be poured back over the meat, which will soak it all up.

5 The meat can now be used for a whole range of dishes from BBQ sandwiches, burger toppings, and wrap fillings to stews, soups and rich curries. Personally I like mine served simply in a sandwich roll – delicious!

To save some for another day, it can be frozen for up to 3 months in suitable containers or freezer bags. Make sure to date it before freezing!

Serves: 20-25

- 4-5kg flat brisket, unrolled
- 1 litre passata
- 150g creamed horseradish (or 100g fresh, grated)
- 20ml Worcestershire sauce
- 5-15ml tabasco, to taste
- 3 celery sticks, washed and cut into chunks
- 100ml vodka
- 2 fresh bay leaves
- Salt and pepper to season

tomato

Wenlock Edge Farm

"Ours is another story of diversification. We started with pigs, and we've stayed with pigs, but now we cure and process, producing a huge range of cures and cuts, including our delicious 12-18 month matured prosciutto. Our Swiss family heritage has helped us appreciate the value of really good charcuterie – we are a small family business and now we have a third generation involved. Interesting fact: a pig is an animal in the genus Sus, within the Suidae family of even-toed ungulates and the only part you can't eat is the squeal!"
Peter and Alison Themans

Pan Roast Breast of Shropshire Pheasant, Wrapped in Wenlock Edge Prosciutto

Served with Black Pudding Purée, Honey Roast Shallots and Kale

1 For the pheasant, remove all skin, sinew and fat from the breast. Next lay two layers of cling film on your bench in a criss-cross pattern then lay two to three pieces of prosciutto overlapping neatly in the middle of the cling film, creating a rectangle slightly larger than pheasant breast, place pheasant breast at one side of rectangle, season with salt and pepper. Next use the cling film to roll the prosciutto around the breast carefully into a log shape, then tying a tight knot at the end of each side of the cling film roll to hold the pheasant prosciutto log in place. Repeat with each other breasts. Leave for two to three hours to shape.

2 For the black pudding purée, dice black pudding into cubes. Poach in cider with sugar and mace for 5-10 mins. Blend until smooth in blender for 10 mins, add more cider if too thick. Add crème fraîche, pulse until fully incorporated. Pass through a fine sieve and season to taste.

3 For the shallots and kale, peel shallots keeping top and tail intact so that the shallot stays whole. Poach in lightly seasoned water gently until soft and translucent, then drain fully so they are completely dry. Melt 75g butter in frying pan until golden brown, add oil then cooked shallots, honey and thyme, fry on medium heat until golden on all sides, stirring regularly. Add other 25g of butter to pan, melt then add chopped kale stir in thoroughly and cook for 1-2 mins. Season to taste

4 To finish pheasant, remove pheasant from cling film rolls carefully. Add oil to large oven proof frying pan over medium heat, once hot, fry on all side until golden, turning regularly. Place pan in oven at 180°C (160°C fan) for 10-15 mins, rotating each breast every 3-4 mins, once cooked remove pan from oven. Add butter, thyme, garlic, baste breasts for 5 mins in brown butter, garlic and thyme. Remove breasts from pan onto a board to rest for a further 5 mins, whilst they rest, use the frying pan with the meat juices, butter, etc. to create the sauce by added the 30ml of cider and 15ml of vinegar, reduce over medium heat until syrupy. Season to taste.

5 To plate, dot black pudding purée over plate, spoon on shallots and kale, slice prosciutto wrapped pheasant and lay over kale and shallots, drizzle over pan sauce.

Tip – this recipe can be done with most small game birds or even guinea fowl or chicken. The quality in this dish lies in carefully cooking the pheasant so that it stays moist and tender, using good quality prosciutto for that artisan cured meat flavour, and using artisan high quality black pudding, to give a creamy and indulgent purée with aromatic spicy flavour.

Serves: 4
- 4 pheasant breasts (young hens often best for this style of dish, hung for a week, ask your local butcher)
- 8-12 rashers of Wenlock Edge Farm Prosciutto
- 30ml extra virgin rapeseed oil
- 80-100g butter
- 3 sprigs thyme
- 3 garlic cloves, crushed lightly
- 30ml cider
- 15ml cider vinegar

For the black pudding purée:
- 250g Wenlock Edge Black Pudding
- 60ml local cider or good quality apple juice
- 20-50g creme fraîche (depending on black pudding consistency when cooked)
- ½ teaspoon ground mace
- 1 teaspoon brown sugar

- 100g small shallots or pearl onions
- 100g butter
- 50g honey
- 4 sprigs of fresh thyme
- A drizzle of rapeseed oil
- 6 stalks of kale, stalks removed and finely sliced (preferably Dwarf Green Curled variety or Red Russian, as the thin leaves cook quickly to retain nutrients and flavour)

pheasant

The King and Thai

"I pride myself on the freshness of my flavours, aromas and the 'fragrance' of my food. This is largely as I make all my pastes and marinades to order, source meats and other products locally and even grow my own Thai herbs. This dish was inspired by the great quality of produce that's on my doorstep – especially during wild mushroom season when I love to go foraging. As a restaurateur, I have great relationships with my suppliers – including my local butcher. He'll often come to the restaurant to tell me what he has in stock, I particularly love his Shropshire beef – it is fantastic! Our customers however are sourced from all over the UK!" **Suree Coates**

Beef with Mushroom in Oyster Sauce

1 For the spring rolls, stir fry garlic and mushrooms in the oil. Add oyster sauce, water and sugar. Taste and season to suit. Leave to cool. Hold back some of the ingredients to place on top of the steak at the end. Divide the mixture in half, wrap in the spring roll skin and shallow or deep fry until golden.

2 Marinade the beef in the oyster sauce for at least 1 hour. Add the cooking oil to the pan and heat. Add the beef – your pan should be really hot. Cook to your preference.

3 Heat up remaining stir fry ingredients and spring roll. Use the garnish to make the plate look beautiful, and serve.

Tip – Don't be afraid to adjust the dish to suit your own palate. For instance, you might decide to use a greater selection of mushrooms, or add different garnishes. As with other dishes, you can turn the heat up by simply adding more pepper and garlic. If you want a more savoury and intense flavour, add a little more oyster sauce.

Serves: 2
- 250g fillet beef, per person
- 1 teaspoon cracked black pepper
- 4 tablespoons oyster sauce
- 1 tablespoon cooking oil
- Shaved carrot, radish and raw mushrooms as option for decor.

For the spring rolls:
- Spring roll pastry, size 215mm x 215mm (called 'skin' available from most oriental specialists)
- 250g mixed mushrooms – wild are best if you can find them – but be careful to pick the right ones!
- 1 clove garlic
- 3 tablespoons oyster sauce
- 1 tablespoon cooking oil
- 1 teaspoon sugar
- 2 tablespoons water

Shropshire's Own

"Our award winning shop has a passion for local food. We started as an online shop and success soon overtook us as we looked for an outlet. The opportunity arose when our village shop and post office became available. We were quick to move in and stock the shelves full of the bounteous Shropshire produce alongside our own homegrown veg, rare breed (Shropshire and Badger Faced) lamb and free range eggs."
Duncan and Sarah Ellson

Serves: 6
- 2kg leg of lamb
- 3 cloves garlic
- 2 sprigs rosemary
- 50g butter
- 750g potatoes, peeled and diced
- 1 tablespoon whole milk
- 1 bunch wild garlic leaves
- 400g tomatoes on the vine
- 2 tablespoons balsamic vinegar
- 2 tablespoons rapeseed oil
- 2 bundles asparagus
- A drizzle of rapeseed oil
- 1 pinch coarse salt

For the mint sauce:
- 1 large bunch mint, chopped
- 3 tablespoons cider vinegar
- 1 teaspoon caster sugar
- 1 large pinch salt
- 1 tablespoon hot water

Roast Leg of Lamb

Served with Wild Garlic Mash, Roast Tomatoes, Asparagus and Homemade Mint Sauce

1 For best results, the lamb needs to rest at room temperature for about 1 hour before cooking. Preheat the oven to 190°C (170°C fan). Using a sharp knife, make some small incisions over the surface of the lamb (just big enough to fit your fingertip into). Finely dice (or crush) one clove of garlic and mix into 20g butter. Rub the garlic butter all over the lamb, working it into the incisions. Finely slice the other 2 cloves garlic and insert a slice of garlic and a little rosemary into each incision. Place in a roasting tin and cover with foil. Pop in the oven for 30 mins, then remove the foil and pop back in the oven for a further 1 hour. The accompaniments can be made whilst your lamb is cooking. For perfect results check the internal temperature of the lamb (63°C for medium-rare, 71°C for medium and 77°C for well done). Allow the lamb to rest for at least 15 mins before carving.

2 For the garlic mash, cover the chopped potatoes with cold water and place over a high heat to bring the boil. Reduce the heat to maintain a simmer, cover and cook for 20 mins, until soft. Drain off the water, and quickly add 30g butter and milk. Mash until smooth. Finely slice the wild garlic, stir in and season to taste.

3 For the tomatoes, mix the balsamic vinegar and oil together and pour over the tomatoes in a small roasting dish. Season with salt and pepper, and roast for about 15-20 mins until cracking.

4 For the asparagus, toss the asparagus in a little rapeseed oil, sprinkle with a little coarse salt and spread evenly over a lined baking tray. Roast in the oven for 10 mins.

5 Homemade mint sauce is so simple and way better than anything you can find in a jar! Simply mix the chopped mint with the vinegar, sugar and salt and hot water.

The Shropshire Spice Company

"When our little company was started 40 years ago in our village pub by a group of locals looking to start a foodie business, little did we think that our idea to offer lightweight, easily-posted products would become such a success. Still trading and still with the same values, the Shropshire Spice Company has a dedicated team of long term staff. Our products are designed for our friends and family – if they like them, then they will definitely be good enough for our customers too! Even our customers help to tweak our recipes."
Fiona Mulroy

Serves: 4
- 40g Shropshire Spice Swahili African Curry Spice Mix
- 1 tablespoon olive oil
- 500g skinless chicken breasts, diced
- 400g can coconut milk
- 400g can chopped tomatoes

For the chapatis:
- 600g plain flour (plus extra for kneading)
- 475ml warm water
- 1½ teaspoon salt
- 100ml vegetable oil

Shropshire Spice Swahili African Curry and East African Chapatis

1 In a large pan heat the oil and fry the chicken until golden. Add the Swahili Spice Mix and fry for a further 2-3 mins.

2 Add the coconut milk and tomatoes and simmer over a medium heat for 25-30 mins, stirring occasionally until the sauce has thickened and the chicken is thoroughly cooked through.

3 To make the East African chapatis, place the flour, salt, 3 tablespoons of the oil and half of the water in a large mixing bowl. Mix well, and keep adding the remaining water until dough becomes soft. Knead the dough for 10-15 mins, add more flour if needed.

4 Divide into 12 equal balls, then cover with cling film so they don't dry out. Roll out each of the balls into a disc about ¼ centimetre thick (don't worry if it is not perfectly round). Brush a little oil on the top, roll the dough circle into a rope, then create a spiral (or coil) with the rope. Place the spirals back under the cling film. Repeat until all the balls have been made into spirals.

5 Take each of the spirals and roll again into a flat circle about ¼ centimetre thick (use flour to prevent the dough from sticking).

6 Heat a non-stick pan on medium heat. Place each chapati into the heated pan. After about a minute, the bottom should be golden and the top translucent, flip it over. Brush a little bit of oil on the top of the chapati, flip the chapati over again, now brush the oil on the second side of the chapati, and turn it over again. After about 30 seconds remove the chapati from the pan and put it on a plate and cover with foil. Repeat for each chapati.

Serve with… rice and a sprinkle of fresh chopped coriander.

Churncote Farm Shop, Butchery & Café

"We have a truly mixed farm with arable, beef cattle, sheep, pigs and poultry. The farm has been in our family for 3 generations and our farm shop diversification showcases our home reared produce. Our shop is in one of our original 18-tie cowsheds. Once a year the Salop Steam Rally comes to our farm – this is one of the largest steam rallies in the world and with over 1000 vehicles on display; it is a sight to behold." **David Clarke**

Slow Cooked Belly of Pork

Served with Potato Rosti, Braised Red Cabbage and a Sweet and Spicy Jus

1 For the belly of pork, score and rub the rind with oil and sea salt. Roast in a hot oven at 200°C (180°C fan) for 25-30 mins, reduce heat and continue to cook on low at 160°C (140°C fan) for 2-3 hours, cover with foil if browning too much. Test if the meat is done, as it should pull apart easily. Allow to rest.

2 For the braised red cabbage, place the cabbage, onion, apple, garlic, red wine vinegar, cinnamon, nutmeg, cloves and sugar in a large pan. Add 3 good knobs of butter, place over a medium heat and cook until tender (about 20 mins), stirring regularly. Transfer to a oven dish, cover and pop into the oven until ready to serve.

3 For the potato rösti, in a tea towel, ring out the grated potatoes and onion to remove excess liquid. Once drained place in a bowl and add the thyme leaves, chopped garlic, salt, pepper and plain flour. Mix all the ingredients together and shape to form a rösti. In a hot frying pan with oil, brown off each side of the rösti and place in hot over for 25 mins to finish cooking.

4 For the sweet and spicy jus, add red wine, beef stock, brown sugar, mixed spice to a pan, heat and reduce until thick and glossy.

Stack the rösti, pork and braised red cabbage high on the plate. We like to serve ours with simple baked apple slices. Top with pork crackling and finish with a drizzle of the jus.

Serves: 6-8
- 1.5kg boneless pork belly
- Olive oil
- Good pinch of sea salt

For the braised red cabbage:
- 1 red cabbage, thinly sliced
- 1 onion, chopped
- 2 apples
- ½ teaspoon cinnamon
- ½ teaspoon grated nutmeg
- ¼ teaspoon ground cloves
- 5 tablespoons red wine vinegar
- 3 tablespoons brown sugar
- 3 knobs butter

For the rösti:
- 4 medium potatoes, peeled and grated
- 1 large onion, peeled and grated
- 2 sprigs thyme, chopped
- 2 garlic cloves, chopped
- 1 tablespoon plain flour

For the sweet and spicy jus:
- 175ml red wine
- 300ml beef stock
- 2 tablespoons brown sugar
- 1 teaspoon mixed spice

The Armoury

"The history of our multi-award winning pub is most interesting, although the food in its previous incarnations was definitely not the talking point it is today. In the 18th century the armoury was producing munitions, although it originally wasn't situated on its present site at all. The whole building was moved lock, stock and barrel (to use an appropriate metaphor) in 1922, from the Armoury Gardens to the banks of the River Severn, because immediately after the First World War, building materials were so hard to come by they recycled what they had. It has served various other purposes in its life, having most recently been a bakery. But now, we are joined by many who feel it is having its best incarnation as our riverside pub restaurant." **Emily Waring**

Rabbit and Prune Faggot

Served with a Cider and Tarragon Jus and Sautéed Wild Mushrooms

1 Pulse the diced rabbit in a food processor and place into a clean bowl, then add pork mince, minced calves or pork liver, mustard, roughly diced prunes, breadcrumbs and set aside.

2 In a pan lightly cook with a little olive oil, diced onion, crushed garlic and then cool down. Add the onions to the faggot mixture mix with the beaten egg, chopped parsley, thyme and a little seasoning. Chill the mixture before rolling.

3 Roll the meat mixture into 80g balls. Place on a tray and chill. Now in a hot non-stick frying pan sauté the faggots in a little oil until golden brown, then place the faggots in a large casserole dish.

4 In a saucepan, lightly sauté in a tablespoon of olive oil, diced onion, crushed garlic sweat down without colour, add the cider and tarragon reduce down by two thirds then add the demi glace/gravy and add the game glace. Then pour the sauce over the faggots and braise in the oven, making sure the tray is covered with foil. Cook for 1 ½ hours on 140°C (120°C fan). Once cooked remove the faggots from the cooking liquor, pass the remaining sauce into a fresh pan and set aside ready for serving.

5 Rinse off the soaked split peas, gently cook in vegetable stock with sprigs of thyme until they are cooked but still have a little bite and set aside.

6 Deep fry the sage leaves and fry off the very thinly sliced parsnips. Sauté the wild mushrooms off in a little butter and olive oil.

Spoon the warm split peas in the bowl, place on the hot faggot pour a little sauce over the top and around the edge. Garnish with the sautéed mushrooms, crispy sage leaves and parsnip shard.

Serves: 6-8

For the faggot mix:
- 500g diced rabbit
- 250g pork mince
- 250g calves or pigs liver diced
- 125g diced streaky bacon
- ½ tablespoon whole grain mustard
- 75g diced pitted prunes
- 50g breadcrumbs,
- 1 egg
- 1 small diced onion
- 1 garlic clove, crushed
- 1 tablespoon chopped parsley
- ½ tablespoon chopped thyme
- Sea salt and milled black pepper

For the braising sauce:
- 500ml cider
- 2 diced onions
- 2 litres good quality beef jus or demi glace
- 2 tablespoons game glace (Essential Cuisine) or a reduced chicken stock pot
- 5 sprigs of tarragon

For the split peas:
- 250g split peas, soaked overnight in cold water with a teaspoon of bicarbonate of soda
- 500ml vegetable stock
- 3 sprigs of thyme
- 2 sliced garlic cloves

For the garnish:
- 200g mixed wild mushrooms
- Sage leaves
- Parsnip, sliced thinly lengthways

Old Downton Lodge

"Our beautiful hotel is housed in old farm buildings, some of which were listed in the Domesday book. Our 'museum' is the most mysterious room of all. Its huge cider press can still trundle powerfully around its stone trough but yet has no drain to let the cider out! Meanwhile we serve regular tasting menus from our restaurant, including delicious local produce alongside wild salads, berries and fungi which our chef Karl forages from nearby woods and fields." **Willem Vlok**

Duck, Celeriac, Damson

1 First, prepare the duck. Remove the legs and place to one side, then run your knife either side of the back bone gently pull the breast away running the knife along the rib cage, taking as much meat off as you can. Once both breasts are removed, place in them in the fridge ready for cooking later.

2 Submerge the legs in duck fat in a deep tray, cover with tin foil and place in the oven at 110°C (90°C fan) (or on the bottom shelf of an Aga) for around 2 hours or until tender.

3 Wash the celeriac and trim the bottom off so it has a nice flat base. Mix the salt and the egg whites together to form a thick paste. Once mixed, cover the celeriac with the paste, and bake on an lined tray at 190°C (170°C fan) for 45 mins until tender. Once cooked, remove the dried paste and discard. Trim the sides of the celeriac with a knife and place in a blender with a touch of water until smooth. Pass through a sieve and set aside. Cut the remaining celeriac into 1cm x 4cm x 4cm squares and set aside.

4 Place the damsons in a pan with a touch of water, cook over a gently heat to allow the damsons to soften. Once they are soft, pass through a fine sieve into a saucepan and add the sugar. Cook until the sugar dissolves. Blend and pass again through a sieve.

5 Make a simple reduction by heating chicken stock in a pan, until reduced by half. Add the red wine and cook out until the liquid has reduced into a silky sauce. Then season to taste.

6 Season the duck breasts, place skin side down in a cold pan. Heat without oil until the skin is nice and crispy then add the cubed celeriac, flip the duck over and add a good knob of butter and baste. Remove from the heat and leave to one side to rest the meat.

7 While the duck is resting, place the celeriac purée on the stove to heat through. Then simply season the hearts and pan fry in a hot pan, with a little oil, for just a couple of minutes.

8 Slice the duck breast and hearts lengthways, they should be nice and pink. Arrange on the plate with the tender confit leg. Add your sweet damson purée and finish with the chicken stock and red wine reduction. ENJOY.

Serves: 2
- 1 wild duck
- 200g duck fat
- 1 celeriac
- 700g salt
- 3 medium egg whites
- 125ml light chicken stock
- 125ml red wine
- 200g fresh damsons
- 1 tablespoon sugar
- 2 duck hearts
- A drizzle of olive oil
- Salt and freshly ground pepper

Duck

The Clive

"The Earl of Plymouth's Oakly Park Estate surrounds the village of Bromfield and extends to some eight thousand acres just north of Ludlow. A royal forest in past times, Oakly Park was purchased by Clive of India in the second half of the 18th century and, although it is not certain that he ever lived here himself, the property has remained in the family through six generations since that time. Hence the name of our establishment, where as far as possible we use ingredients from our estate including seasonal vegetables grown in Lady Windsor's Walled Garden. Our bread, cheese, jams and pickles are handmade at the estate's award winning Ludlow Food Centre right next door. Localism is definitely on our agenda!"

Pork Belly, Bean Stew and Pomme Purée

1 For the pork belly lay the washed and dried pork belly in a deep tray lined with greaseproof paper. Pour over the vegetable oil, season with salt and thyme. Cover with the lid and place in the oven at 170°C (150°C fan). Cook for 3-4 hours until meat is falling apart and completely cooked. Leave the pork to cool before cutting into desired portion sizes.

2 For the bean stew, place a medium sized pan on a high heat and pour in the sunflower oil. Once hot, add the onion, carrot, streaky bacon lardons and crushed garlic. Reduce heat and sweat. Add the haricot beans, stock, tomatoes and bouquet garni. Proceed to cook on a low heat until the beans are tender. Leave to one side until needed. Just before serving, add the freshly chopped herbs and any desired seasoning.

3 For the pomme purée, place the potatoes and sprig of thyme into a pot, covering with cold water. Place on a high heat and bring to boiling point. Once boiling, strain out 70% of the water. Place a lid on top and steam until cooked through.

4 Before the potatoes are cooked, put the cream, butter, salt and pepper into another pot. Bring to a simmer and remove from the heat. Leave to one side until needed. Once the potatoes are cooked, remove the sprigs of thyme and drain the water. Mash the potatoes and add the cream mixture until the desired consistency has been reached.

We serve ours with a simple pork jus, a sprinkle of micro herbs and a curl of crispy pork crackling to finish!

Serves: 4
- 1kg Ludlow Food Centre Gloucester Old Spot Pork Belly, bone removed
- 2.5 litres vegetable oil
- 700g haricot beans
- 1 onion
- 1 carrot
- 2 tablespoons sunflower oil
- Bouquet garni
- 5 cloves of garlic, peeled and crushed
- 8 tomatoes, peeled and chopped
- 1.2 litres stock
- 225g Ludlow Food Centre Unsmoked Streaky Bacon, cut into lardons
- 500g Maris Piper potatoes, peeled and chopped
- 250ml Mawley Milk Single Cream
- 50g Ludlow Food Centre Unsalted Butter
- Salt and pepper
- Several sprigs of thyme
- Parsley and tarragon, washed

The Coach & Horses

"The Shropshire Sheep is the oldest pedigree sheep bred in the UK, with the Shropshire Sheep Society being founded in 1882. As the head chef of our beautiful 16th century coaching inn, and Masterchef quarterfinalist, I am passionate about using the best local and seasonal produce. And I am pleased to share that passion with my suppliers like Sarah Crow of Crows Agricultural, who supply us with amazing Shropshire lamb. I love her passion and dedication. She is always striving to produce the very best lamb possible and started farming Shropshire Sheep after two ewes were given to her and her husband Dorian in 1996 as a wedding gift!" **John Barton**

Roasted Rack of Herb Crusted Shropshire Lamb

Served with Spring Vegetables and Shrewsbury Sauce

1 Preheat the oven to 200°C (180°C fan). Heat the rapeseed oil in a non-stick pan until hot. Season the lamb well with salt and pepper and put into the pan fat side down with a sprig of rosemary. Once the meat is golden brown and nicely seared, turn the lamb over and seal the other side off. Just before removing from the pan add a little butter to the pan and baste the meat with it. Remove from the lamb from the pan and place in a roasting dish fat side up.

2 To make the herb crust for the lamb, place the white breadcrumbs and all the herbs in a food processor and blitz until fine, season with salt and pepper.

3 Spread a thin layer of Dijon mustard over the fat on the lamb. Top with the herb breadcrumbs which will stick to the mustard and hold them in place.

4 Place the lamb in the oven and cook for 10-12 mins until medium rare (for well done or medium adjust cooking times by an extra 5-10 mins) when the lamb is done remove from the oven and allow it to rest for at least 5-10 mins before serving.

5 For the spring vegetables, bring a pan of water to the boil. Blanch all the vegetables in the water for about 5 mins then refresh in iced water to stop the cooking process, set aside until just before serving.

7 For the Shrewsbury sauce, heat the lamb stock in a pan until hot. In a separate pan reduce the red wine down by at least half to the consistency of a glaze, add the redcurrant jelly, rosemary, tomato purée and the hot lamb stock. Reduce to the consistency of a sauce and season well with salt and pepper and a squeeze of fresh lemon juice.

8 To serve, place the rested lamb rack on a wooden carving board. Reheat the spring vegetables in a little butter with some chopped fresh tarragon and serve in a bowl on the side of the lamb. Pour the Shrewsbury sauce into a jug and serve on the side.

Serves: **2**

For the lamb:
- 1 rack of Shropshire Lamb, French trimmed
- 1 tablespoon Dijon mustard
- 150g white breadcrumbs
- 1 tablespoon fresh rosemary, chopped
- 1 tablespoon fresh tarragon, chopped
- 1 tablespoon fresh thyme, chopped
- 1 tablespoon fresh parsley, chopped
- 2 tablespoons good quality, cold pressed rapeseed oil
- 1 tablespoon unsalted butter
- Maldon Sea Salt
- Freshly ground black pepper

For the spring vegetables:
- 8 asparagus spears, trimmed
- 100g freshly podded peas
- 100g freshly podded broad beans
- 8 baby carrots, washed but tops left on
- 1 tablespoon finely chopped fresh tarragon
- 1 tablespoon unsalted butter
- Maldon Sea Salt
- Freshly ground black pepper

For the Shrewsbury sauce:
- 450ml good quality homemade lamb stock
- 1 sprig of fresh rosemary
- 1 tablespoon redcurrant jelly
- 1 teaspoon tomato purée
- 150ml good quality strong red wine
- ½ teaspoon lemon juice
- Maldon Sea Salt
- Freshly ground black pepper

The Olive Tree Restaurant

"Although the Olive Tree Restaurant is based within the Holiday Inn Telford/Ironbridge (part of the internationally renowned IHG chain of hotels), where our guests might be anticipating a standardised approach to the menu, our restaurant is anything but. We have a strong commitment to delivering the very best dining experience for all our guests. My brigade of chefs is highly trained and passionate about the dishes we create. We believe in sourcing our food locally, that's why we have built close relationships with local suppliers and farms, ensuring we understand the journey of our ingredients. To be able to tell the story behind the food we produce is very important to us, and supporting the local economy is part of our ideology. Our dishes change with the seasons and therefore deliver the freshest taste possible." **Nigel Davis**

Duo of Cherrington Farm Beef

Braised Blade and Flat Iron Steak, with Buttercross Farm Smoked Bacon and Cabbage Parcel, Creamy Mash, Butternut Squash Purée, Baby Carrots, Courgettes and Asparagus

1 Vacuum pack the blade of beef with 150ml beef stock, fresh thyme and seasoning. Cook in a water bath for 15 hours 80°C. Remove from bag, set aside cooking juices to later add to the sauce. Shred beef and split into 4 portions, mould beef into a sausage shape, wrap in caul fat and keep warm. Vacuum pack flat iron beef with 150ml beef stock and seasoning. Cook in a water bath for 26 hours 57°C.

2 Place the carrots into a bag with the carrot juice and cook in a water bath 1 hour 45 mins at 88°C.

3 For the primo cabbage parcels, blanch 4 cabbage leaves for 2 mins in hot water and refresh in cold water. Sauté strips of smoked bacon and shredded cabbage. Fold mix into cabbage leaf, vacuum pack and keep warm in water bath until serving.

4 Remove the flat iron beef from the bag, set aside cooking juices to add to the sauce. Pan sear the outside to caramelise and colour. Rest and slice.

5 For the sauce, put wine into pan and reduce by half, add stout and reduce further, add cooking juices, stock and Demerara sugar.

6 For the mashed potato, boil the potatoes, drain, dry and pass through a strainer. Add butter, cream and fresh herbs. Season to taste.

7 For the butternut squash purée, boil the diced butternut squash until tender, then blend with the butter and season.

8 For the asparagus, trim and steam for 3 mins. For the courgettes, shape into a barrel with a turning knife, steam for 3 mins. Season to taste.

9 Place a swoosh of butternut squash purée on the middle of the plate, add the blade of beef in centre and pipe mashed potato around the beef. Arrange slices of pink flat iron steak on top. Garnish with cabbage parcel baby vegetables, add sauce and serve with a glass of red wine.

Serves: 4

- 500g blade of beef
- 500g flat iron beef
- 300ml beef stock
- A piece of caul fat
- Fresh thyme
- Salt and freshly ground pepper
- 16 baby carrots
- 100ml carrot juice
- 1 primo cabbage
- 200g smoked bacon
- 200g asparagus
- 1 courgette

For the sauce:
- 60ml stout
- 60ml red wine
- 570ml beef stock and cooking liquor
- 1 teaspoon Demerara sugar

For the butternut squash purée:
- 1 butternut squash, peeled and diced
- 100g butter
- Seasoning

For the mashed potato:
- 680g potatoes, peeled
- 30g butter
- 60ml cream
- Fresh herbs and seasoning

Meat from Cherrington Farm and Buttercross Farm. Vegetables from AJ Edwards, Chadwell Grange Farm and Canalside Farm.

Fordhall Organic Farm

"Our farm is family run and community-owned. It has been worked by the Hollins family as tenant farmers for generations. Saved from developers in 2006 through a high profile campaign, which raised £800,000 through the sale of £50 not-for-profit shares, we founded the first community-owned farm in England. Fordhall Farm has been organic for over 65 years, our cattle and sheep graze out on pasture year round and all our produce is sold direct to the public. Our café and farm shop live inside our lovely eco-buildings. Our aim is to reconnect consumers to their food through experiences including free trails and events; giving an opportunity for all to learn about the food cycle first hand." **Charlotte Hollins**

Feeding A Crowd, All Year Round

Slow Cooked Shoulder of Pork with Rosemary, Juniper and Organic Cider Marinade

1 Blitz the juniper berries, fennel seeds, rosemary, salt and pepper in a processor, gradually adding oil to loosen to a runny paste. Rub this marinade all over the pork, cover with cling film and refrigerate overnight.

2 Preheat oven to 220°C (200°C fan). Trim and halve your onions or leeks and the garlic bulb and place in the bottom of a deep roasting tray. Place the pork joint on top, fat side up; add any marinade and juices that have come off the pork. Roast for 25-35 mins until the skin is nicely golden and fat is starting to render. Remove from oven, pour the cider into bottom of tray and cover tray with a double layer of foil. Turn the oven down to 180°C (160°C fan) and roast for a further 5-6 hours until the meat is easily pulled apart with a fork.

3 For extra crunchy crackling, remove the pork from the tray, strip off the skin, scrape off any excess fat and place on top of a cooling rack over a roasting tin and return to the oven until it starts to crisp (it will crisp up more as it cools.) The pork can be wrapped in foil and rested while you do this.

In Spring – Bircher Potatoes, Asparagus, and wild Garlic Sauce: Scrub 1 baking potato per person, cut in half short ways. Place in a roasting tin, cut side down. Butter or beef dripping will work best – use 3 tablespoons, dotted around the potatoes, sprinkle with salt and black pepper. Bake at 200°C (180°C fan) for 45-50 mins. The cut side will be golden and crispy like a roast potato whilst the top's are fluffy like a jacket potato. Blanch 3-4 bunches of asparagus in boiling salted water for 2-3 mins, quickly remove from water and toss with unsalted organic butter, salt and pepper. Blitz a handful of foraged wild garlic leaves into some thick yoghurt and season with black pepper and a drizzle of rapeseed oil.

In Summer – Chargrilled Little Gems, Broad Beans and Herb Yoghurt Dressing: Cut 1 little gem per person in half lengthways, keep the core intact. Lightly brush with rapeseed oil, chargrill for 3-4 mins to lightly colour all sides of the lettuce. Place into a serving bowl. Blanch 1kg podded broad beans in boiling water and quickly plunge into ice cold water. Remove the skin to reveal the bright green beans. Scatter these over the little gems. Blitz some pouring yoghurt with soft summer herbs (basil, dill, marjoram, dill, parsley, mint, tarragon) a large garlic clove and the juice of a lemon. Drizzle over the salad, sprinkle over some more chopped herbs.

In Autumn – Tray Baked Heritage Squash, Walnuts and Kale: Use a selection of heritage squash varieties, (gem, harlequin, kuri, spaghetti, celebration). Peel, deseed and cut into 2.5cm chunks, toss in rapeseed oil, salt, black pepper, chopped sage and 3 or 4 lightly crushed garlic bulbs. Bake for 35 mins at 190°C (170°C fan), remove, stir in a handful of walnuts and return to the oven for a further 10 mins until the squash is softened and the walnuts have begun to colour. Shred 2 heads of green kale, removing the tougher stems. Blanch for 4-5 mins in rapidly boiling salted water then quickly remove from the pan and plunge straight into cold water. When the tray bake is ready, mix the blanched kale through it, dress with a drizzle of rapeseed oil, balsamic vinegar and season.

In Winter – Jerusalem Artichoke Gratin and Braised Red Cabbage: Thinly slice 3kg scrubbed Jerusalem artichokes and 1kg leeks. Place in a saucepan, cover with 300ml double cream. Add 6 cloves of garlic, 50g thyme and 50g butter, gently bring to the boil. Tip into a greased gratin dish and dot some butter over. Cover with foil, bake at 180°C (160°C fan) for 90 mins, remove the foil and return to the oven for a further 15 mins to brown. Remove the outer leaves from 1 red cabbage, cut into quarters, remove the core. Finely shred and place into a pan with 1 tablespoon cider vinegar, 250ml apple juice, 1 teaspoon salt, 1 teaspoon sugar, 1 cinnamon stick and 2 star anise. Core 2 cooking apples, finely slice and add into the pan. Mix well and cover the pan with foil. Cook on a low heat for 40-50 mins, add more apple juice if it dries out.

Serves: 8-10
- 4kg Gloucester Old Spot pork shoulder, boned and rolled with the skin scored
- 2 tablespoons juniper berries
- 2 tablespoons fennel seeds
- 2 large sprigs of rosemary
- 1 bottle of organic cider
- Sea salt and black pepper
- British rapeseed oil
- 1 head of garlic
- 4-5 red or yellow onions, or 2-3 leeks

The centrepiece of this recipe is a delicious slow roasted, tender joint of free range Gloucester Old Spot pork. At Fordhall our food is always seasonal. This recipe can be adapted throughout the year by using the best seasonal, British vegetables.

Great Berwick Organic Longhorn Beef

"Our family has been farming at Great Berwick since 1949 and we specialise in producing, what we believe to be, some of the finest most flavoursome, organic, pasture fed Longhorn Beef in the country. Our herd of beautiful cows graze the organic, clover rich meadows next to the River Severn. Happy and content in their relaxed, completely stress free surroundings, our cattle mature slowly and naturally under our care. We use our own cold room to dry age all our beef on the bone for 5 weeks. This allows the meat to develop a rich dark colour with a fantastic depth of flavour. We're passionate about how we farm, how we butcher, how we prepare and how we offer the very best of British Beef." **Claire and Sam Barker**

Please note that a simple meat thermometer is essential.

Over cooking slow grown, dry aged meat is a real shame, as everything the producer has done to reach this stage has been with a view to presenting you with tender, juicy meat with tonnes of flavour.

Regardless of whether your roasting joint is on or off the bone, or its size, plan ahead! Using this method you need to allow between 8 and 24 hours cooking time.

The Ultimate Roast Beef, Hassle Free!

We have learnt, through trial and error, a fail safe way to cook our Roast Beef (that is, if you like it pink in the middle). It's also great if you're unsure as to what time you are going to serve, as the meat will be at its optimum for a good length of time.

1 Heat your oven to 220°C (200°C fan). Take the meat out of the packaging and allow it to reach room temperature. If you're using Great Berwick Organics Longhorn Beef, you'll notice that some areas are much darker than others, these will be areas of meat that have been exposed to the air for up to 5 weeks. When cooked, these are actually the yummiest bits of all.

2 Put the meat (uncovered) into the hot oven for approx. 15 mins. This does several things; it adds colour and flavour to the outside of the meat by crisping it up. Secondly it helps seal in the moisture. Thirdly it starts a chain reaction through the enzymes which weaken and tenderise the meat.

3 After the 15 min 'sizzle', take the meat out of the oven, reduce the temperature to 50°C (no less than 48°C and no more than 56°C) which is easier said than done, as most ovens don't register this on the dial! We find the best way to achieve this is to place a meat thermometer in a mug of water and then in the oven. Turn the oven dial to where you think 50°C is (as it's often not where you think it might be), give it a few minutes and then check the reading and adjust up or down accordingly. Once you know where the dial needs to be you can trust that for future cooking.

4 Place the meat in the oven uncovered for between 8 and 24 hours or until the core temperature of the meat has reached between 48°C and 56°C. Don't worry there's no danger of the meat overcooking at this temperature. Just before you serve it, give it another 10 min blast in a hot oven.

Allow to rest for 10-15 mins and then carve and enjoy! We love ours simply with Yorkshire puddings, horseradish sauce, and seasonal veggies.

The Hundred House

"Our awards speak for themselves. Not many restaurants can boast 2AA Rosette Awards, representing great quality food, for 18 years consecutively! We are here to stay. Sheila our pastry chef has been with us for the full 28 years and on last estimate she has cooked around 42,000 portions of the world's best treacle tart – sweet! We are also very proud that we buy 70% of our produce from within a 30 mile radius." **Stuart Phillips**

Apple Smoked Duck and Duck Confit Croquette

Served with Roast Beetroot, Horseradish Cream and Rainbow Chard

1 For the duck breast, first make the brine one day ahead. In a saucepan, sweat the vegetables and herbs gently (without colour) for 15 mins. Roast the spices at 180°C (160°C fan) for 5 mins in a tray. Add the herbs and spices, salt, sugar and water to the pan, bring to a simmer for 45 mins, then chill. Pour the brine over the duck breasts and leave overnight in the fridge.

2 The following day, remove duck breast from liquid, pat dry with clean cloth, then smoke over apple wood for 1.5 hours in a Bradley or similar style smoker.

3 For the duck confit croquettes, preheat the oven to 210°C (190°C fan). Warm the duck legs in the oven for 2-3 mins. Remove the skin and finely slice, then sweat in a small frying pan over medium heat, cooking until crisp. Remove and drain on a paper towel. Debone the legs and put the meat with a small glass of water in the frying pan. Cook slowly over low heat until the liquid has evaporated. Shred meat with fork, set aside.

4 Wash and finely chop the mushrooms. Place the olive oil in the frying pan with the shallots, cook until golden brown. Season generously and add the cream. Cook for 2-3 mins, then pour into a bowl and set aside. Add the shredded duck meat, skin and chives to the mushroom mixture. Adjust seasoning to taste, cover and place in the fridge until cool.

5 Beat the eggs in a bowl. Lightly flour your hands then shape small amount of the duck and mushroom mixture into croquettes by rolling between the palms of your hands. Coat in the egg then roll in the breadcrumbs. Coat again in eggs and breadcrumbs. Place in the fridge.

6 To finish, place duck breasts, skins side down in a dry frying pan over a low heat. The gentle heat will render the fat from the breast and brown the skin. After a few minutes turn over and place in oven for 5-8 mins at 185°C (165°C fan). Rest in a warm spot for at least 6 mins. Meanwhile bake croquettes at 185°C (165°C fan) until golden.

To serve… cut croquettes in half and serve thinly sliced breast with roast beetroot, chard, potato purée, horseradish cream and duck jus.

Serves: 6-10

For the brine:
- 2 large white onions, peeled and chopped
- 2 large carrots, peeled and chopped
- ½ head of celery, chopped
- 3 garlic bulbs, split, peeled and chopped
- 8 allspice berries
- 8 cloves
- 1 tablespoon coriander seeds
- 1 tablespoon whole black peppercorns
- 1 tablespoon fennel seeds
- 20g thyme
- 6 bay leaves
- 45g coffee beans
- 630g salt
- 220g sugar
- 5 litres of water
- 1 duck breast per person

For the duck confit croquettes:
- 2 confit duck legs, approx. 600g
- 100g button mushrooms
- 2 teaspoons finely chopped French shallots
- 2 tablespoons olive oil
- 250ml whipped cream
- 1 teaspoon finely chopped chives
- 2 eggs
- Plain flour, for dusting
- Breadcrumbs, for coating
- Vegetable oil, for deep frying

Green Fields Farm Shop

"Our farm shop has been going since 1990, and in 2007 we also opened our online shop, using our distinctive carrot van to deliver free to our local customers across Telford and Newport. The shorter the distance our food has travelled the fresher it's bound to be, consequently over 80% of products are from the best, and most passionate producers within a fifty mile radius. From corporate lunches and business menus to local household supplies, everything we sell also comes with a smile from our friendly happy workers." **Natalie Walker**

The Green Fields BLT

1 The air dried tomatoes need to be done at least a day in advance. Slice tomatoes lengthways in half and lay on a cooling rack placed inside a tray. Drizzle with the oil and scatter the herbs, garlic and seasoning as evenly as you can over the tomatoes. Leave uncovered somewhere warm for at least a day. Once ready, you can either serve that day or keep sealed and covered in oil to preserve.

2 For the chorizo and tomato relish, peel and dice the chorizo then cook gently to release the oil. Drain and place into another clean pan. Add the rest of the ingredients and cook gently until almost all of the liquid has gone. Be sure to stir often. Once cooked blend to a smooth paste.

3 To make the mustard mayo, simply add the mustard to the mayonnaise and mix well, until combined.

4 For the vinaigrette, place the shallots, garlic, vinegar, sugar and mustard. Blend until smooth and then with the blade still running, slowly pour in the vegetable oil and then the sunflower oil. Continue blending for a few more seconds and then pour into an airtight container until needed.

5 To finish the sandwich, cook the bacon (for best results use a chargrill like we do).

For each sandwich, spread one slice with the mustard mayo and the other side with the chorizo and tomato relish. I usually place the lettuce onto the mayo side to 'stick' it to the bread, then the tomato on top. The lettuce prevents the tomato juice from making the bread soggy. Top with the chargrilled bacon and then the chutney side of the bread.

Serves: 2
- 6 slices Wenlock Edge bacon
- Dressed lettuce, preferably baby gem
- 4 thick slices of fresh homemade bread

For the air-dried tomatoes:
- 5 plum tomatoes
- 1 teaspoon fresh rosemary, chopped
- 1 teaspoon fresh thyme, chopped
- 2 garlic cloves, thinly sliced
- Olive oil
- Sea salt and cracked black pepper

For the chorizo and tomato relish:
- 5 small Wenlock Edge chorizo sausages
- 10 fresh tomatoes, cut into eighths
- 2 teaspoons ground coriander
- 1 teaspoon ground cinnamon
- 200g light brown sugar
- 200ml red wine vinegar
- 200ml red wine
- 2 red onions, chopped
- 2 garlic clove, chopped

For the mustard mayo:
- 1 teaspoon Mikes Gourmet Mustard
- 1 tablespoon mayonnaise

For the vinaigrette: (makes 710ml – but keeps well)
- 2 banana shallots
- 3 garlic cloves
- 100g light brown sugar
- ½ tablespoon Mikes Gourmet Real Ale Mustard
- 125ml white wine vinegar
- 284ml sunflower oil
- 284ml vegetable oil

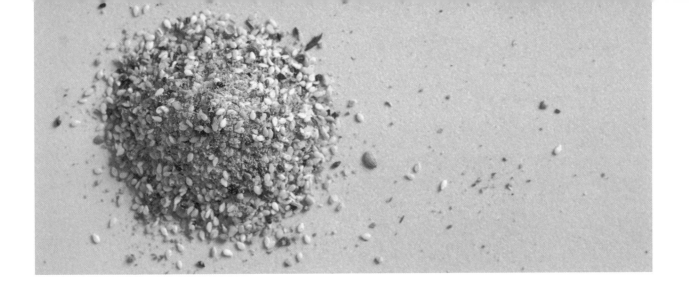

Cooking Like Cleopatra

"I love my native country of Egypt. While I grew up in Germany, I spent some formative parts of my childhood with my father's family in Naga Hammadi, a small village north of Luxor, and also in Cairo and Alexandria. My passion for Egyptian food was largely inspired by my beloved Aunty Mouneira; she taught me all about Egyptian cooking. Now I have decided to share my family magic with Shropshire and beyond. Some of my recipes date back to those of the ancient pharaohs but I can assure you, they still taste as fresh and as mouth-wateringly good! Using local ingredients and flavouring them up with Egyptian spices and herbs, my signature recipes bring a little bit of Luxor to Ludlow and the mix is superb – just like Shropshire!"
Marina Ibrahim

Ful Medammes

Hearty fava bean stew – the Shropshire way

Egypt's national dish – you don't know Egypt, until you try Ful Medammes. This nutritious fava bean stew is traditionally eaten for breakfast or as street food snack.

1 In a pan of boiling water cook the fava beans for 10 mins. Meanwhile, heat the oil in a frying pan with the chilli, onions and the coriander, sauté for 2 mins until they release aromas, add the bell pepper, stir and cook for another 2 mins.

2 Drain the fava beans and add into the frying pan, mix everything together, then pour into a bowl.

3 Crush the beans with a fork, add the tahini, season with salt, pepper and cumin, add squeeze of lime juice and mix well. Finally sprinkle the Cleopatra's Dukka on top.

Serve with... pita bread, pickled vegetables and spring onions.
Bil hana wa shifa – Enjoy!

Serves: 2
- 250g fava beans (or indigenous broad beans)
- 1 tablespoon rapeseed oil
- ½ chilli, finely diced
- 1 small onion, finely diced
- ¼ bunch fresh coriander, chopped
- ½ bell pepper, diced
- 2 tablespoons tahini (sesame paste)
- A squeeze of lime juice
- A pinch of ground cumin
- Salt and freshly ground pepper
- 1 tablespoon Cleopatra's Dukka

Ludlow Food Festival

"When our Festival started over 20 years ago, the aim was to promote the very best food and drink of the Marches area. Today we still remain true to that original focus and we think that is what makes it unique. Several of the producers who took a chance and booked a space that very first time have returned year after year. Father and son, Jim and Nick Davis had only established Hobsons Brewery two years previously when they charmed visitors to the first Festival with their generous samples served in proper glasses. Now a hugely successful company regularly winning regional and national awards, Hobsons still share our values by standing by a strong ethos of sustainability, community and passion for quality, craft and provenance. Family businesses feature strongly at the Festival. Swifts the Bakers, based at Clee Hill, with a shop and bakery school in Ludlow, not only have a stall showcasing their artisan breads, but Robert, a fifth generation baker, gives bread-making demonstrations and hands-on masterclasses.

Our Exhibitor Bursary is awarded to carefully selected businesses, who might be too small or too new to afford to trade at the Festival. This bursary enabled Sam and Claire Barker of Great Berwick Organics to introduce their organic Longhorn beef to our visitors, they were so overwhelmed by the enthusiastic response that they have never looked back.

Whether they have been with the Festival since the beginning, have joined along the way, or are new kids on the foodie block, it is the passionate, dedicated food producers who make the Ludlow Food Festival the special event it is." **The Ludlow Food Festival Team**

Marches Fondue

A fondue is a wonderfully informal way of entertaining. This version includes Oakly Park Cheddar made at Ludlow Food Centre with milk from the estate's own herd of Friesan-Holstein cows. The cheese is combined with cider from Oldfields Orchard, a new branch of the Hobsons family.

1 Rub the inside of the fondue pot with the cut side of the onion. Place the cider and lemon juice in the pot and heat gently, on top of the stove, until bubbling. Gradually stir in the grated cheese and heat gently, stirring, until completely melted. Tip – Take care not to overheat the cheese while it is melting.

2 In a small bowl, blend together the cornflour, mustard powder and apple juice. Stir into the cheese mixture. Continue to cook, gently, stirring until thick and smooth. Stir in the sage, season with salt and pepper then transfer the fondue pot to a lighted burner.

To serve… spear apple and bread onto fondue forks to dip into the fondue, and serve with bresaola.

Serves: 6
- ½ small onion
- 300ml Oldfields Orchard medium dry cider
- 1 teaspoon lemon juice
- 450g Oakly Park Cheddar, grated
- 1 tablespoon cornflour
- Pinch mustard powder
- 3 tablespoons Appleteme apple juice
- 1 teaspoon chopped fresh sage
- Salt and freshly ground black pepper

To serve:
- Wedges of apple
- Cubes of Swift's baguette
- Slices of Wenlock Edge Farm bresaola

Passionate puddings, naughty nibbles and divine drinks

Bacheldre Watermill

"Our mill was first recorded in 1575 as part of an Elizabethan estate. It was rebuilt in 1747 and we arrived recently in 2002 to maintain and use it. Much of our equipment dates back to these early days and still produces the finest quality flour possible. The bottom stone is the bed stone which stays still and then the top stone known as the runner stone. At approximately 4 feet wide and weighing nearly a ton, balance is paramount. The grain is slowly ground to retain the natural goodness of the wheatgerm. This process just slightly warms the flour leaving all the natural flavours intact. Great flour, makes great baking!"
Matt and Anne Scott

Fennel Seed Lavash Crackers
Served with Fennel Jam and Shropshire Blue Cheese

1 For the fennel jam, mix all ingredients in a pan and cook on medium heat, stirring regularly, until sticky and golden. Season and chill.

2 For the lavash crackers, mix all the dry ingredients, in a mixer with a dough hook, gradually add in the melted butter, milk, and eggs (one at a time) until it all forms a dough. Knead for 10 mins, until it becomes stretchy. Place in the fridge for 2 hours to rest.

3 Remove and roll flat on lightly floured bench, sprinkle the crushed fennel seeds over one half and fold over so the seeds are in the middle of the dough, then roll out to less than a 1mm thick (easiest done through a pasta machine but ok with a rolling pin). The dough should be almost see through.

4 Cut the dough into the long cracker shapes and lightly oil with rapeseed oil. Bake in a preheated oven at 180°C (160°C fan) until golden brown, this should take approx. 8-12 mins, but keep one eye on it!

Serve the lavash cracker and fennel jam with your favourite local cheese, we love a good blue, like Ludlow Blue or Ironbridge Blue.

Makes: Lots (but saves well!)

For the fennel jam:
- 500g fennel bulb, chopped into very fine dice, (this can be done using pulse on a food processor)
- 80g butter
- 100g golden caster sugar
- 350ml white wine
- 150ml cider vinegar
- 3 sprigs of thyme, leaves only
- 3 star anise
- Salt and freshly ground pepper

For the lavash crackers:
- 500g Bacheldre Watermill Strong White Flour
- 200g Bacheldre Watermill Spelt Flour
- 200g Bacheldre Watermill Wholemeal Flour
- 12g salt
- 15g icing sugar
- 100 butter, melted
- 350ml milk
- 2 whole eggs
- 1 egg yolk
- 15g fennel seed, crushed

Tip – Raw dough can be frozen for future use, only roll out what is needed.

Merangz

"We use only local, free range eggs for our delicious Merangz, and we separate each and every one by hand. This is unlike other producers who use liquid egg white with no provenance! Our "egg project" then packs the yolks and sells them country-wide to professional chefs and caterers. Bringing a little sophistication to Shropshire, the cosmopolitan flavours and colours of our Merangz include everything from passion fruit to pistachio, and mocha to lime. Something you may not know is that slow baked meringues are still referred to as "pets" (translation: farts!) in the Loire region of France due to their light and fluffy texture!"
Leanne and Brian Crowther

Eton Mess Merangz with White Chocolate Ganache Filling

A wonderfully straight forward summer dessert classic, the Eton Mess Merangz is a delicious hand separated free range egg meringue bite made with a natural strawberry flavour, drizzled with Belgian white and strawberry chocolate, and finished with raspberry crumble.

1 Place the chocolate into a medium sized microwave safe mixing bowl. Set aside while you heat the cream. Slowly heat the cream and butter in a small saucepan until just boiling.

2 Pour the cream over the chocolate and leave to stand for 2 mins, this will give the chocolate time to soften. Stir the ganache until smooth. If all the white chocolate has not melted then place the bowl in the microwave and heat for 30 seconds. Remove and stir until smooth.

3 Leave the ganache to cool at room temperature for 10 mins. Whilst cooling set a piping bag with a number 10 nozzle. Once the ganache has cooled and thickened slightly, spoon into the piping bag. Insert the nozzle into the base of each Eton Mess Merangz Bite – squeeze gently until the bite is full of ganache.

Serve immediately – arrange bites on a plate, with raspberries and finish with sprig of mint. The ganache will set over time – these too are equally delicious!

Serves: 4
- 12 Eton Mess Merangz Bites (or 4 giants)
- 200g white chocolate
- 100ml double cream
- 75g unsalted butter
- A punnet of raspberries
- Sprig mint to garnish

raspberry

Mikes Homemade

"I started beekeeping in 2012 as wanted to add honey to my Mikes Homemade product range, and so began my fascination with bees and their plight. Honey has many uses and has been used by humans from as early as 7000BC, when honey was the nectar of the gods, bees are fascinating creatures, the all female worker bees spend their lives looking after the queen, foraging for nectar and pollen, within a 3 mile radius of their hive, with a natural built in 'sat nav', so they will always find their way home." **Mike Denith**

Shropshire Honey Cake

Serves: 6-8
- 250g Mikes Homemade Runny Honey (plus a little extra for glaze)
- 225g unsalted butter
- 100g light muscovado sugar
- 3 duck eggs (or 3 large chicken eggs)
- 300g self raising flour

1 Preheat oven to 160°C (140°C fan). Line a 20cm cake tin, with a removable base. Cut the butter into small pieces and place into a pan with the honey and sugar. Melt slowly over a low heat, until mixture looks like liquid, then bring to boil for approx. 1 minute.

2 Put mixture to one side to cool for 15-20 mins (its important to allow to cool, so the eggs are not cooked when mixed in). Beat the eggs into the melted honey mixture, using a wooden spoon.

3 Sift the flour into a large bowl and then stir in the eggs and honey mixture, beating until you have a smooth and runny mixture. Pour the mixture into your prepared cake tin. Cook for 50 mins to 1 hour, until well risen, and a skewer pushed through the middle comes back clean.

4 Place the cake on a wire tray, melt a couple of tablespoons of honey and drizzle over the top to glaze. Allow to cool

Why not treat yourself to a slice, with a scoop of clotted cream and a couple of strawberries, for the perfect afternoon tea treat?

Toot Sweets Chocolates

"I started producing high quality chocolates after returning to Shropshire after working as a Department Manager in the Grocery and Confectionery departments at Selfridges. My passion for local food and confectionery comes from my mother who was a keen cook. I pride myself on using only the finest quality chocolate which has been ethically sourced. My chocolates have won awards from the British Academy of Chocolate and the International Chocolate Awards. It takes 3-5 years before the Theobroma Cacao (cocoa tree) bears fruit. Each tree produces around 1000 beans per year which is enough for 1kg of chocolate. The average Brit eats 11.5kg of chocolate a year." **Julia Wenlock**

Chocolate Salted Caramel Fondant with Chantilly Cream

1 Break the chocolate into small chunks, add to a pan with cubes of the butter and melt slowly until the mixture is fully melted and combined. Take the pan off the heat.

2 In a bowl gently whisk the eggs and sugar together, you want the eggs and sugar to be combined, but not fluffy. Slowly pour the egg and sugar mixture into the pan and whisk the mixture together, then add the flour and mix until smooth and set aside.

3 Brush 4 dariole moulds (or ramekins) with the melted butter and dust with cocoa powder, making sure the cocoa powder coats the sides of the moulds. Fill each mould one third full and refrigerate for 30 mins. After 30 mins the mixture will have set, pop a Salted Caramel into the middle of the ramekin (top of the chocolate facing down, and the flat bottom facing up), and top the ramekin up with the rest of the mixture, leaving a 1-2mm edge. Make sure you clean the rim of the ramekin using a cloth or your finger as this will help you later when you take the fondant out of the ramekin. Chill the fondants for 1 hour. You can also make these fondants the day before if you're holding a dinner party.

4 Split the vanilla pod and scrape out the seeds. Pop the seeds into a bowl with the cream and icing sugar. Whip until the cream just thickens.

5 Preheat the oven to 180°C (160°C fan). Cook the fondants for 9 mins, serve immediately, turning the fondants out on to the serving plate and serving with Chantilly cream.

When you cut into the fondant the centre will be a mixture of salted caramel and gooey chocolate.

Serves: 4
- 85g butter
- 75g good quality chocolate (I've used a 65% Vietnamese Chocolate by Marou, really delicious rich chocolate flavour)
- 3 medium free range eggs
- 75g golden caster sugar
- 70g plain flour sieved.
- 4 Toot Sweets Salted Caramels

For the moulds:
- 25g butter, melted
- 25g cocoa powder

For the Chantilly cream:
- 100ml double cream
- 1 tablespoon icing sugar
- 1 vanilla pod

chocolate

Chilton Liqueurs

damson

"The wonderful old damson orchards of Shropshire are the source of the Shropshire prune damson which I slowly steep in Greenall's London Dry Gin. Local damsons were originally grown not for food, but for their strong coloured dye and were widely used in the local carpet industry and for naval uniforms. My husband and I are both born and bred in Shropshire and feel lucky to have been able to bring up our family in the beautiful Welsh Marches. We are also both delighted to be to able to promote this wonderful county by producing our Shropshire made range of gins and vodka." **Fiona Rogers-Coltman**

Chilton Cocktail Trio

Purple Lady
Serves: 1
- 50ml Chilton Damson Gin
- 20ml fresh lemon juice
- 20ml Cointreau
- 1 egg white

Dry shake all ingredients hard in a cocktail shaker (to get the egg white to froth), then shake with ice. Serve in a coupe glass. Garnish with a mint leaf on foam.

Raspberry Daisy
Serves: 1
- 50ml Chilton Raspberry Vodka
- 15ml fresh lemon juice
- 20ml grenadine
- 50ml pineapple juice

Shake hard in a cocktail shaker with ice, and strain over crushed ice in a tall sling glass. Garnish with citrus peel shavings.

Breakfast Martini
Serves: 1
- 50ml Chilton Seville Orange Gin
- 1 teaspoon marmalade
- 3 teaspoons honey
- 100ml pink grapefruit juice

Shake in a cocktail shaker with ice. Strain into a martini glass with a grapefruit wedge garnish.

Taste of Shrewsbury

lemon

"We are proud to have an established coffee shop in Shrewsbury. An ancient and historic market town with a largely unaltered medieval street plan with over 660 listed buildings, Shrewsbury serves as the commercial centre for Shropshire and mid Wales with a huge commercial output. So we have a captive audience of plenty of happy customers who come to taste our varied and delicious juices, sandwiches cakes and unusually flavoured scones. It's a family affair and working with husband and sons means we are never far apart. It's a family affair!" **Kay Crane**

Lemon Cheesecake with Blueberry Coulis

1 Lightly grease a 20cm round, loose bottom cake tin. Mix together the ingredients for the base and spread over the bottom of the prepared tin.

2 Separate jelly into squares. Dissolve in 150ml boiling water, then add the juice of the lemon to make up to 300ml. Put into a cool place until jelly is thick and nearly set.

3 Mix the soft cheese with the sugar and almost set jelly and then fold in the whipped cream. Turn into the tin on top of the crumb base and cool in fridge.

4 For the decoration, cut the pared rind into very fine strands. Blanch in boiling water for 1 minute. Rinse under cold water. Dry thoroughly on kitchen paper.

5 Transfer the cheesecake out onto a plate and pipe cream around top of cheesecake.

6 For the blueberry coulis, pop the berries, caster sugar and water into a pan, bring to the bill and heat for 5 mins until softened, stir in the vanilla essence, then blend to a purée in food processor. Pass through a sieve to remove pulp. Refrigerate.

Serves: 12

For the base:
- 200g digestive biscuits, crushed
- 100g butter, melted
- 60g castor sugar

For the cheesecake:
- 600ml packet lemon jelly
- Juice from one lemon
- 350g soft cheese
- 100g castor sugar
- 150ml whipping cream, whipped

To decorate:
- 150ml whipping cream, whipped
- Pared rind from one lemon

For the blueberry coulis:
- 250g blueberries (or wild Shropshire whimberries)
- 50g golden caster sugar
- 100ml water
- ½ teaspoon vanilla extract

A Nice Slice Of Cake

"My beautiful whole sponges are handmade and home baked with care, perfect for sharing! I use local free range eggs and lashings of jams and curds made using fruit from a local farm. No colours, no icing, no stress, just seasonal flavours from nature, with a dusting of sugar. In history the practice of inviting friends to come for afternoon tea was picked up by Queen Victoria who regularly used to dress up for the occasion. I wonder if she would have liked my classically English Elderflower and Gooseberry?" **Julie Francesca Mynard**

Serves: 8-12

For the gooseberry jam:
- 1kg gooseberries, topped and tailed
- Juice of ½ lemon
- 1kg granulated sugar

Tip – Gooseberries are naturally high in pectin so you don't need to use specialist jam sugar for this.

For the sponge:
- 225g fair trade caster sugar
- 225g soft margarine
- 4 free range medium eggs
- 225g sifted self-rising flour
- 2 tablespoons elderflower cordial

For the butter icing:
- 250g unsalted butter
- 275g icing sugar, sifted

Elderflower and Gooseberry Naked Sponge

1 For the gooseberry jam, first sterilise your jars by washing thoroughly in very hot soapy water. Rinse in very hot water then put on a baking sheet in a 140°C (120°C fan) oven until completely dry.

2 Put the gooseberries, lemon juice and 400ml water in a large wide pan (use a preserving pan if you have one). Bring to the boil then simmer for 15 mins until the fruit is very soft and pulpy. Put 2 or 3 small saucers in the freezer (these will be used to test the setting later on). Add the sugar and stir over a gentle heat for another 10 mins until the sugar is completely dissolved. You don't want it to boil at this point as the sugar could crystallise. Once you can't feel or see any grains of sugar bring to the boil and boil hard for 10 mins, skimming the surface as you go and stirring now and again to stop it catching.

3 Spoon a little jam onto a chilled saucer, leave to cool then run your finger through it. If it's ready it will wrinkle up. If this doesn't happen boil for another 5 mins then keep testing and boiling until it does. Do a final skim on the finished jam then pour into the sterilised jars and seal. Store in a cool dark place – the jam will be good for up to 6 months. Keep in the fridge once opened.

4 For the sponge, place caster sugar in a bowl with the soft margarine and beat until mixed and smooth. Stir in the free range eggs making sure the batter is not lumpy. Add the elderflower cordial to taste. Beat in the sifted self-raising flour until the sponge mix is smooth. Place the sponge mix equally into two cake tins that are lined with greaseproof paper. Bake for 25 mins at 180°C (160°C fan). Remove the cakes from the tins and place on a wire rack to cool completely.

5 For the butter icing, beat together the butter and icing sugar until soft and smooth.

6 Once the cake has cooled, you can now assemble it. Take the two halves of the cake and decide which will be your bottom layer and which will be your top. I prefer to spread the butter cream on first and this needs to go on the lower half of your cake. Next spread the gooseberry jam on top of the butter cream. Place the other half of your cake carefully on top. Dust with a little caster sugar and decorate with elderflowers.

Appleby's Cheese

"My grandparents-in-law started our cheese business in the stable next to the kitchen. Lance milked the cows and Lucy made the cheese. Unlike other cheese makers who wax their cheese, ours is cloth bound to allow it to breathe and mature. In the 80s my parents, Edward and Christine used to load the Landrover full of cheese and take it to London to sell, now we sell it worldwide. Cheshire cheese was even mentioned in the doomsday book – ours is unusually made with raw milk, rubbed and turned daily." **Sarah Appleby**

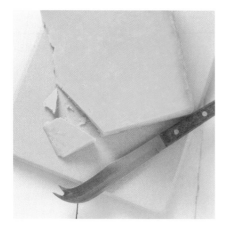

Serves: 8

For the filling:
- 8 large apples, peeled, cored and sliced 1cm thick
- 1 lemon, zest and juice
- 150g brown sugar
- 3 tablespoons corn flour
- ½ teaspoon fine sea salt
- 1 teaspoon ground cinnamon
- 75g unsalted butter

For the cobbler topping:
- 250g plain flour
- 75g spelt flour
- 50g cold butter
- 110g granulated sugar
- 2 teaspoons baking powder
- ½ teaspoon fine sea salt
- 250g Appleby's Cheshire cheese, grated
- 1 egg, beaten
- 250ml cold buttermilk (or more if needed)

Appleby's Cheshire Cheese and Apple Cobbler

1 Preheat the oven to 190°C (170°C fan) and grease a deep, 30cm round, baking dish.

2 For the filling, stir the brown sugar, corn flour, salt, and cinnamon together in a large bowl. Add the apples and lemon zest, toss to evenly coat. Gently stir in the lemon juice. Let the apples sit for 15 mins to release some of their juices, stirring occasionally. Tip the contents into the prepared dish. Cut the butter into small cubes and scatter over the apples. Cover the dish tightly with foil and bake on the bottom rack of the oven for 20 mins.

3 For the cobbler topping, cut the butter into the flour in a large bowl, until it resembles coarse crumbs. Add the sugar (keeping a tablespoon reserved), baking powder, and salt and stir. Add the Appleby's Cheshire cheese (reserving a little) and toss until evenly coated. Make a well in the centre of the bowl and add the buttermilk and beaten egg. Stir just until the dry ingredients are moistened. The dough should be shaggy and moist. If the dough seems too dry, add a bit more buttermilk, a tablespoon at a time.

4 Take the baking dish out of the oven and remove the foil. Divide the dough into about 9 even, round cobbles, place the cobbles evenly on top of the apples. Sprinkle the remaining tablespoon of sugar over the biscuits, along with a reserved sprinkle of Appleby's Cheshire cheese.

5 Return the cobbler to the oven (without the foil) and bake for an additional 30 mins, or until the apples are tender, the juices are bubbling, and the cobbles are puffed and golden brown.

Serve warm with a spoon of crème fraîche.

This is best served the day that it is made, but any leftovers can be wrapped in cling film and kept at room temperature for 2 to 3 days.

apple

Acton Scott Historic Working Farm

"Our historic working farm, run by Shropshire Council, offers a fascinating insight into rural life at the turn of the 19th century. As farm life unfolds daily and the land around is worked by heavy horses, providing a picture of life as it might have been on a Victorian country estate. Farming was an integral part of life in Victorian times. In 1937, when Queen Victoria came to the throne, a third of the working population of Great Britain worked in the countryside. Compare that to less than 1% now involved in agriculture – that's why we need to educate our young about farming, its roots and its future. Our lovely café housed in the estate's old school house serves up delicious food, often using some of the produce from the farm" **Mathew Poulton**

Acton Scott Pear Tart

1 First make the pastry. Put the flour in a bowl, add the butter and rub in with your fingertips until the mixture resembles fine breadcrumbs (or do this in a food processor). Stir in the sugar, salt and cinnamon, and add enough cold water to bring the mix together into a medium-firm dough that is not too sticky (you'll probably need 50ml or thereabouts). On a floured surface, shape the dough into a round, wrap in cling film and chill in the fridge for 30 mins.

2 Heat the oven to 200°C (180°C fan) and grease a large baking tray or line it with baking parchment. Peel, quarter and core the pears, then cut each quarter into two. Heat the butter and sugar in a pan and, when bubbling, add the pears. Cook gently over a medium heat for a few minutes, until the pears are just tender and you have a bubbling toffee sauce. Drain the pears in a sieve, retaining all the sauce. Cool the sauce in the fridge for later.

3 For the frangipane mixture, cream the butter and sugar together until fluffy. Add the egg, flour, almonds and vanilla, and beat well.

4 Roll out the pastry to a large, rough-edged circle no thinner than 4mm and place on the tray. Spread the frangipane over the pastry, leaving a 2cm border clear around the edge. Arrange the cooked pears on top, then sprinkle with the demerara sugar and flaked almonds. Bake for 20 mins, until the pastry is golden brown at the edges. Allow the tart to cool for 10-15 mins, then serve with fresh pouring cream!

Delicious!

Serves: 8-10

For the pastry:
- 250g plain flour
- 125g cold unsalted butter, cut into small cubes
- 50g caster sugar
- Pinch of salt
- A pinch of ground cinnamon (optional)
- 50ml cold water

For the pears:
- 4 barely-ripe pears
- 2 tablespoons soft brown sugar
- 50g butter
- 1 tablespoon demerara sugar
- 1 tablespoon flaked almonds

For the frangipane:
- 75g soft butter
- 75g caster sugar
- 1 large egg, lightly beaten
- 20g plain flour
- 75g ground almonds
- A dash of vanilla extract

Shrewsbury Flower Show

"Shows and pageants, such as the early Shrewsbury Flower Show, which was originally called the Gooseberry and Carnation Fair, were introduced into Shrewsbury in the early 19th century as a way of bringing new business and income to the town. Country people living in the surrounding areas had no real need to leave their village regularly because each had its own range of local tradesmen who could produce almost everything which they needed. The first 'Shrewsbury Flower Show' was held on 29th July 1875 and has been held every year since with the exception of the war years and is the World's longest running independent Flower Show. Today as well as the stunning floral and horticultural aspects, it features T.V. personalities, celebrity Chefs, singers and spectacular arena acts entertain the crowds for 12 hours on each day of the show, ending with a magnificent firework display." **The Shropshire Horticultural Society**

Strawberry and Lavender Pannacotta with Basil and Violets

1 To make the strawberry and basil compote, simply purée 100g of the strawberries with the icing sugar and dice the remaining 100g of strawberries and mix these together. Thinly slice the basil leaves and mix these into the strawberry mixture and set aside.

2 Start making the pannacotta by soaking the gelatine leaves in cold water. Warm the cream, lavender sprigs, caster sugar and vanilla seeds together in a pan before whisking in the softened gelatine leaves. Take off the heat and when cooled slightly whisk in the 50g of strawberries which have been puréed. Pour into 4 small glasses and leave in the fridge for at least 4 hours to set.

3 To make the shortbread crumble place all of the ingredients into a large bowl and rub the mixture between your fingers until you have a breadcrumb like consistency. Scatter the mix over a baking tray lined with parchment and bake in the oven at a moderate temperature for around 15 mins or until the shortbread starts to turn a light golden brown. Leave to one side to cool.

4 To construct the dessert, firstly top the set pannacotta with the shortbread crumble before spooning over the strawberry and basil compote. Whip together the cream, sugar and vanilla seeds and pipe small peaks on top of the strawberries. Finish the dessert with beautiful sweet violets.

Serves: 4

For the strawberry compote:
- 200g strawberries
- 20g icing sugar
- 4 fresh basil leaves

For the pannacotta:
- 400ml whipping cream
- 50g strawberries
- 110g caster sugar
- 2 sprigs of lavender
- 2 leaves of platinum gelatine
- 1 fresh vanilla pod

For the shortbread crumble:
- 170g plain flour
- 60g caster sugar
- 110g butter
- 10 lavender buds

To garnish:
- 100g whipping cream
- 10g icing sugar
- 1 vanilla pod deseeded
- 4 violet flowers

Lavender

The Shropshire Spirit Co.

"My background is not classically one that would suggest a career in artisan food or drink! I've worked on ISAs in a well known building society and as a teaching assistant at Wrekin College. I now take pride in creating fabulous spirits from scratch. I combine the exotic flavours of the Caribbean with the rural delights of Shropshire for deliciously smooth results. My gin and vodka are redistilled through local fruits and other botanicals for tasty and pure flavours." **James Crone**

Summer Rum Smoothie

A refreshing, ice cold smoothie with fresh berries

Keep it simple: Put all of the ingredients together in a blender and blitz it up. Then serve over ice.

A little more: Crush the berries in a pestle and mortar, drain the juice and discard the seeds and skins. Crush the ice and shake everything together in a cocktail mixer. Strain and serve over ice.

Serves: 2
- 30ml Fabulously Salopian White Rum
- 15ml Fabulously Salopian Raspberry Vodka
- 30g cherries
- 30g raspberries
- 30g blueberries
- 30g blackberries
- Dash of elderflower cordial
- 1 teaspoon honey
- 100g ice

The Raven Hotel

"Our hotel has been providing hospitality to Shropshire folk and many beyond for over 300 years. And our head chef Jason Hodnett has represented the central region on BBC2's Great British Menu in 2014 and 2015. Every item we serve at the hotel from ice-cream to bread, from the crispy pig's ears to the British spelt risotto – everything is made on the premises. Our attention to detail has earned us 2 AA Rosettes, and we are aspiring for more! You may have even seen us on the big screen… if you have ever seen the film 'Clockwise' starring John Cleese you will note that the telephone scene was filmed on the site of the Raven's kitchen! Our moment in the spotlight!" **Team at The Raven**

The 'Sweet Shop'

1 For the ice cream, separate 5 egg yolks into a mixing bowl. Add the caster sugar and whisk on a medium speed. Heat the milk, cream and parma violets over a medium heat to bring to the boil. Once boiled, slowly incorporate liquid into eggs whilst continuing to whisk. Return mixture to pan and cook over a low heat until thickened resembling a custard consistency. Churn for 15-20 mins.

2 For the marshmallow, on a medium speed start whisking egg whites. Add caster sugar, liquid glucose, banana foams and water to a pan and bring to the boil. Heat the sugar to 118°C and allow to cool. Soak the sheeted gelatine in cold water and when soft stir into sugar liquid at around 65-68°C. When the egg whites have started to soft peak slowly pour the sugar in, and increase speed to high. At stiff peak continue to whisk for a further 4 mins until glossy. Line a baking tray with baking parchment and leave to set at room temperature for 24 hours.

3 For the meringue, start by whisking egg whites on a medium speed. Mix caster sugar and icing sugar together. When foamy, add a table spoon of the sugar at a time. Once sugar is dissolved into meringue, add the bubble gum flavour drops, continue to gain a stiff peak. Fill a piping bag with your meringue mixture and pipe onto baking trays as desired. Leave in a warm dry place for 24 hours until crisp; alternatively bake at 120°C (100°C fan) for 12-14 mins.

4 For the chocolate marquise, whisk eggs and sugar until pale. Melt chocolate, zest and butter over bain-marie. Slowly add the chocolate to eggs once melted. Sieve cocoa powder over chocolate mixture and fold before adding the orange juice. Line a tray with baking parchment and allow the mix to rest in the fridge for up to 4 hours.

Assemble all the elements together on a plate, however you desire. We cut a round chocolate base, arrange the ice cream, marshmallow and meringue delicately on top, finished with crushed parma violets, alpine strawberries, dots of strawberry conserve and violet petals for decoration.

Serves: 10

For the parma violet ice cream:
- 470ml full fat milk
- 157ml double cream
- 5 egg yolks
- 2 rolls of giant parma violets (80g)

For the banana marshmallow:
- 250g caster sugar
- 50g liquid glucose
- 6 sheets of gelatine
- 100ml water
- 100g banana foams

For the bubblegum meringue:
- 250ml egg whites
- 225g caster sugar
- 175g icing sugar
- 20g corn flour
- 4 x drops bubblegum flavouring

For the chocolate marquise:
- 3 eggs (whole)
- 5 egg yolks
- 300g caster sugar
- 300g unsalted butter
- 125g dark chocolate
- 200g cocoa powder
- 2 oranges, zest and juice

The Tipsy Tart

strawberries

"Everyone loves the name of my company – it's something you can't forget! My drinks are all about having fun, being flirtatious and vibrant so that all my customers 'feel the love', just as I do for my tasty liqueurs. My range is huge – anything can be infused with delicious fruity, chocolatey, or caramelly flavours. It's all about the fun of the making and the joy of the taste – the tipsy tart never disappoints (as the actress said to the bishop!)." **Elizabeth Grinker**

The Tipsy Tart's Apple and Cream Liqueur Sponge with Pink Sunset Cocktail

1 Heat the oven to 180°C (160°C fan). Wash, peel, slice and gently poach the apples to soften slightly. Once softened add to a greased casserole dish which is 22x30cm (or individual tins if you like).

2 Cream together sugar and butter (or margarine) until light and fluffy. Add the eggs one at a time, beating well after each addition. Sift all dry ingredients together and add to the butter mix, a little at a time, alternating with the milk.

3 Pour cake batter over the apples and bake for approx. 40 mins or until a skewer comes out clean.

4 Just before you take the apple pie out of the oven, heat The Tipsy Tart Cream Liqueur until warm. When the apple pie comes out of the oven, poke a few holes into the hot cake and immediately pour over the warm cream liqueur to allow it to soak in.

Serve warm with cream (or ice cream) and a glass of Pink Sunset. To make a Rose and Rhubarb Pink Sunset, simply add The Tipsy Tart Rose Gin and Rhubarb Syrup to a large pitcher, add as many sliced strawberries and raspberries as you like, top with ice. Pour over the Prosecco and stir. Ta da!

Serves: 4-6
For the sponge:
- 200g sugar
- 80g unsalted butter (or margarine)
- 3 large eggs
- 140g self raising flour
- A pinch of baking powder
- A pinch of salt
- 60ml milk
- 4 to 5 cooking apples.
- 200ml The Tipsy Tart's Cream Liqueur

For the Pink Sunset:
- 200ml The Tipsy Tart's Rose Gin
- 200ml The Tipsy Tart's Rhubarb Syrup
- 700ml bottle of Pink Prosecco
- Strawberries
- Raspberries

Café Brulôt – Orange Flavoured Turkish Style Coffee

Many people find Turkish coffee too bitter, but when my parents lived in Turkey, I came across this recipe which was geared to the tourists. The little addition of orange lifts the flavour for the more Western European palates. After finding a similar drink in a classic Viennese Coffee House, with the addition of Cointreau, this provided the finishing touch to the end of all my dinner parties.

1 Whip the cream and add the grated orange rind into the cream. You will not have time at the finish. Reserve a little orange rind for decoration.

2 Place the water in the Ibrik, (a milk saucepan can be used) add the sugar lump and heat the water to dissolve. Stir in all the Aroma Turkish Mystery coffee and then return the Ibrik to the heat. For authenticity a campfire would be ideal!

3 Bring the liquid to the boil so that the coffee froths up, do not allow it to boil over. Remove from the heat and rest for two minutes until the grounds have settled back down. Do this again twice.

4 Once the coffee has frothed up the third time, let the grounds settle briefly and add the orange juice and Cointreau. Then immediately pour into the demitasse cups. Spoon the cream over the top and sprinkle the reserved rind to finish. DO NOT strain the coffee, the grounds will settle to the bottom of the cup. Sip and enjoy!

Serve with… a glass of water and sweet baklava or Turkish delight.

Makes: 4 coffee demitasse cups
- 100ml freshly drawn cold water
- One lump of white sugar
- 20g Aroma Turkish Mystery Pulverised Freshly Roasted Coffee
- 1 orange, finely grated rind and juiced
- 20ml Cointreau
- 2 tablespoons whipped cream

Turkish coffee pots, or "Ibriks" as they are known, are used all the way from Arabia right through to the South Eastern side of Europe, each country in between (with the exception of Austria) claiming it as their own! Ibrik's are small copper saucepan like pots with a tinned lining, a narrow neck and long wooden handle to protect your hands from the heat. This is the only coffee making process which works well with the coffee being boiled. For every other method the old adage "coffee boiled coffee spoiled" is all too true.

Coffee Beans…

Aroma Tea & Coffee Merchants

"Founded over 30 years ago, our coffee roasting company was started when I bought my mother a cafetiere and walked around Shrewsbury looking for fresh coffee beans, to no avail. Freshly roasted coffee has a short lifespan to be at its optimum taste – 4 weeks as a bean or 10 days if ground. Imported from ethical sources and chosen for their unique flavours, our coffees are roasted daily. Our Masteroasters will have soon roasted enough raw coffee to have made one billion cups. That's a lot of coffee!" **Andrew Turner**

Origins Restaurant at Shrewsbury College

"Our new contemporary and commercially run restaurant in Shrewsbury gives our students the opportunity to work in a professional environment and stay ahead of industry trends. Alongside modern practices in cuisine, we are still training our students the skills of the past. Here you can also enjoy table theatre including 'flambé' or 'guerdon' service where food is prepared in front of you. At time of going to press Trip Advisor finds us the 6th best place to eat in Shrewsbury and that's pretty good for a band of students!" **Dan Gibbons**

Serves: 6
- 8 fresh basil leaves
- 100ml raspberry coulis
- 70g brown sugar
- 100ml Chilton's Raspberry Vodka
- 90g egg whites
- 170g light brown sugar
- 40g water
- 500g whipping cream

For the Shrewsbury biscuits:
- 125g butter
- 150g caster sugar
- 2 egg yolks
- 225g plain flour
- Finely grated rind of 1 lemon or orange

For the meringue drops:
- 1 egg white
- 60g caster sugar

Raspberry Vodka and Basil Parfait
Served with Shrewsbury Biscuits and Meringue Drops

1 For the parfait, bring 130g of the light brown sugar and the water to the boil and continue to boil until it reached 115°C. Place the egg whites into a mixing bowl and add the remaining 40g of light brown sugar and whisk until light. When the water has reached 115°C slowly add to the egg white mixture, whilst beating.

2 Add the cream and the fresh basil to a thick bottom saucepan and warm over a medium heat until the flavour has infused into the cream. Remove basil and allow cream to cool. Continue to whisk the water and egg mixture until it has cooled right down, once the mixture has cooled add the coulis and the cream. Once the mixture has been sufficiently mixed, add to desired moulds and place in freezer over night.

3 For the biscuits, preheat oven to 180°C (160°C fan). Cream the butter and sugar together until pale and fluffy. Add the egg yolks and beat in well. Stir in the flour and lemon rind and mix to a fairly firm dough. Knead gently on a lightly floured surface and roll out until about ½cm thick. Cut out 6.5cm rounds with a fluted cutter, and put on greased baking sheets. Bake for about 15 mins, until lightly browned and firm to the touch. Transfer to wire racks to cool. Store in an airtight container, biscuits should last about a week.

4 For the meringue drops, whip the egg whites until stiff. Carefully sprinkle in the sugar, whilst continuing to mix, the mixture should appear to thicken and be able to stand at a peak. Using a disposable piping bag, add the mixture and cut a small (½cm) hole in the end. Pipe the mixture onto greaseproof paper about the size of a small grape.

Bake in the lowest oven temperature possible. The aim is to dry out the meringues without causing any colour.

Assemble all the elements on the plate carefully. We used a simple raspberry sauce, whole raspberries, freeze dried raspberries and basil leaves to create this striking plate.

Shropshire Ice Cream

"Mi place tanto la bella italia! Great culture and lovely people, but you will always find me seeking out the local "gelato" to taste the huge variety of flavours on offer, bringing home many ideas to experiment with. When we start our recipes with locally sourced farm fresh milk and cream; and eggs from free roaming hens, we are already on the way to giving our customers the finest traditional dairy ice cream. Adding the best selection of seasonal fruit and ingredients that Shropshire has to offer results in a delicious ice cream that has a real taste of the region. Each batch of ice cream we produce at The Shropshire Ice Cream Company HQ takes at least 24 hours which gives our customers a luxuriously creamy ice cream to enjoy, but I have experimented with a few different make at home recipes and this one gives the best outcome in a fraction of the time using only 2 ingredients before adding whatever you have in the cupboard or in the fridge." **Pat Parkes**

Easy Peasy Homemade Ice Cream

The enemy of creating a smooth ice cream is ice crystals. It is important if you are making it without an ice cream maker that everything is as cold as possible before you start. I use a metal mixing bowl which I put it in the freezer for an hour which helps to start the freezing process off. If not, before you start put a metal roasting dish in your freezer and have some ice cubes handy.

1 Put all the ingredients into your chilled bowl and whisk until thick and creamy. Put your bowl into your roasting tin and surround it with ice cubes. Place in the freezer.

2 After 30 mins remove from freezer and whisk again. Dot any ripple ingredients onto the ice cream and use a fork to swirl them in, making sure you get to the bottom of the ice cream. Return to your freezer.

3 Your ice cream should be ready to eat after about an hour (depending on your freezer settings). If you are not eating it straight away it can be stored in a plastic tub, but will need to be taken out of the freezer for about 10 mins before scooping.

Having a dinner party? Want to impress your guests?

Why don't you surprise your guests with an "Affogato" – which means "drowned" in Italian.

Affogato is simple to create but a real experience to taste! Put a scoop of coffee ice cream into a small coffee cup then pour about half a shot of fresh espresso coffee over the ice cream for a delicious hot and cold experience! We also "drowned" our lemon ripple ice cream in elderflower liqueur, or you could use a lemon liqueur.

Go crazy with flavour!

Why not try strong flavoured fruits such as raspberries, blueberries and blackberries as they work well in this rich ice cream. Lightly crush the fruit and ripple into the ice cream.

Or how about half a jar of smooth peanut butter or chocolate spread – great rippled in. YUM!

For a Christmas treat, try 1-2 teaspoons of ground cinnamon and half a cup of mixed fruit soaked overnight in a couple of tablespoons of dark rum, folded into the mixture before putting in the freezer.

Enjoy experimenting and hopefully you will fall in love with ice cream as much as me!

It is fun to get children involved with this simple recipe, as well as impressing your friends with your homemade ice cream! You don't even need an ice cream machine, just a hand held food mixer.

Makes: **4 generous servings** (or 3 if my family are visiting!)
- **300ml double cream**
- **½ can of condensed milk (397g size)**

Lemon Ripple:
- **½ jar of good quality lemon curd (plus 2 tablespoons for the ripple)**
- **½ unwaxed lemon, zest**
- **½ teaspoon Limoncello (if you have any from last years holiday!)**

Coffee Cream:
- **2 tablespoons espresso coffee power with 2 tablespoons coffee cream liqueur (optional)**

A small amount of alcohol in ice cream stops ice crystals forming, but be careful you don't add too much otherwise it will never freeze! No more than ½ tablespoon alcohol in this quantity (but a little more if it is a cream based liqueur).

Katie's Kids Kitchen

"I truly believe that the kitchen is the heart of our homes. I am a mother to three wonderful boys whose healthy appetites and desire for cooking and creating in the kitchen, were the inspiration behind my business. Sharing my skills and cookery knowledge with pre-schoolers right through to young adults has been really rewarding. I teach them how to bake, about where our food comes from and the basics of cookery in a fun and exciting way. We even get to eat the fantastic results! There's nothing better than getting little hands to help out in the kitchen, they may even help with the washing up too!" **Katie Wellington**

Trifle of Madness!

1 First make the sponge, preheat your oven to 180°C (160°C fan). Beat together the butter and sugar, add the eggs and flour, beat until smooth. Split mixture into two bowls. Add green food colouring into one bowl and pink to the second bowl.

2 Spread into 2 shallow tins and bake in the oven for 20 mins, or until a wooden skewer comes out clean. Allow to cool.

3 Layer the trifle in a large 3 litre glass bowl, adding whichever layers you like first. We layered green sponge, then fruit, then jelly (allowing it to set). Then pink sponge, followed by the custard, with the cream whipped with blue food colouring on the top. A handful of Smarties topped off the madness.

Serve with… a huge spoon and lots of hungry children. Mad hats are optional!

Serves: **At least 12**
- For the sponge:
- 225g butter
- 225g sugar
- 225g flour
- 4 eggs
- A couple of drops green food colouring
- A couple of drops pink food colouring

For the trifle:
- 2 x 400g tinned fruit (berries/peaches)
- 2 sachets of strawberry jelly
- 1 litre custard
- 600ml whipping cream
- A couple of drops blue food colouring
- A handful of Smarties

eggs

Bank House B&B

"Our Georgian renovation is more than just an architectural jewel – it's a haven for yoga retreats and relaxing stays, or for hearty Shropshire breakfasts and afternoon tea for walkers and cyclists. Knowing what is needed when I've been away on walking holidays with a large group has been key in creating a comfortable, home from home feeling for all our guests. In the winter the log burning stoves and biomass boiler keep everyone cosy, and in the summer guests can enjoy a drink in our peaceful garden. Find us right in the centre of Bishop's Castle (just a stone's throw away from the town hall) and enjoy our large rooms, with sash windows, high ceilings, oak floors and great views across the rooftops of the medieval town."
Gerry Barwell

Bank House Healthy Drink Duo

Spiced Summer Pudding Smoothie
Makes: 2 – but you may not want to share!

- A teacupful of mixed Shropshire summer fruits – e.g strawberries, raspberries, blackcurrants, blackberries
- 1 small banana (preferably frozen – don't forget to peel the banana before freezing)
- 4 dates
- 200ml of organic milk (use semi skimmed or full fat for best taste)
- A good dollop organic natural yoghurt – Greek style yoghurt works well
- 2 teaspoons of Shropshire honey – we use Clun Valley Honey
- A few drops of natural vanilla essence
- Large pinch ground cinnamon
- Large pinch ground cardamom

Chop banana and dates. Put all the ingredients into a blender and blitz. Enjoy.

Zingy Green
Makes: 1 large glass

- Half a cucumber
- 1 stick of celery
- 1 apple
- Large handful of green leaves (spinach, kale or chard are best)
- Slice of lemon
- A thumbnail sized piece of fresh ginger

Put all the ingredients through your juicer to have a green zingy super healthy juice.

Butterbelle

"My nut butters are processed slowly in very small batches, allowing the naturally present oils to be released from the nuts. This creates a soft, smooth texture and avoids the need for the addition of any vegetable oil or palm oil. Nuts have it all in terms of nutrition-they are packed with protein, heart-healthy fats, vitamins, minerals and antioxidants." **Zoe Harrison**

Walnut and Maple Butter Tartlet with Ginger and Honey Ice Cream

1 Begin by making the ice cream. Boil the milk and cream in a saucepan. In a bowl, whisk the sugar and egg yolk, until thick and creamy. Pour the hot milk and cream over the eggs and sugar mix, whisking well. Add the honey and ginger. Pour back into the pan and cook out on a medium heat, continuously whisking until thick. Allow the mixture to cool, then place in the freezer, whisk every 30 mins until frozen (alternatively you can use an ice cream machine, if you have one).

2 For the sweet pastry, mix the butter, icing sugar and salt together with your fingertips. Gradually work in the flour, until a breadcrumb texture is created. Add the eggs, one at a time, working into a smooth dough, knead for a couple of minutes.

3 Rest the pastry in the fridge for 2 hours. Roll out to 2mm to 3mm thick, cut into rounds and put into individual tartlet cases. Rest again in the fridge for 30 mins, then prick the base. Bake blind with baking beans at 180°C (160°C fan) for 30 mins, remove baking beans, and cook for another 5-10 mins until golden brown and crisp. Leave to cool on a wire rack.

4 For the crème Anglaise filling, bring cream, milk, sugar, vanilla to a simmer (do not boil). Whisk into egg yolks, then add the walnut butter. Leave to cool.

5 To finish, pour enough mix into each tart case to fill and bake on a tray at 110°C (90°C fan) for 15-20 mins, or until set. Remove and serve at room temperature with a scoop of the ice cream.

Serves: 8
For the ice cream:
- 400ml double cream
- 400ml milk
- 250g caster sugar
- 10 egg yolks, organic
- 50g honey, local
- 60g stem ginger in syrup, finely diced

For the sweet pastry:
- 250g plain flour
- 100g butter, softened
- 100g icing sugar
- Salt
- 2 eggs, room temp.
- 1 egg yolk, room temp.

For the walnut and maple butter crème Anglaise filling:
- 20ml milk
- 500ml double cream
- 60g caster sugar
- 1 vanilla pod, seeds
- 5 egg yolk, large organic, beaten lightly
- 250g Butterbelle Walnut and Maple Butter

Pimhill Farm

"The course of Pimhill Farm was changed because of a chance remark and the loan of a book about soil fertility from a fellow undergraduate to my father at Glasgow University in 1948. Having already been concerned about soil health, he and my grandfather took the decision to adopt organic farming methods. They did so not because of an existing premium market – but in the belief that it was the right thing to do for the health of the land and the animals. Pimhill Farm has been farmed organically ever since. We grow wheat and oats and have a dairy herd of 260 cows. Fertility is provided by the cows and by crop rotation. Nature and wildlife conservation are top priorities. Today we continue to believe that how your food is grown is important to land, animal and human health." **Ginny Mayall**

Pimhill Organic Flapjacks

1 Preheat the oven to 160°C (140°C fan). Grease and neatly line a 25x25cm baking tin with baking parchment.

2 Melt the butter in a pan with the sugar, syrup and a pinch of salt. Stir well to combine, then take off the heat and stir in the oats.

3 Press the mixture evenly into the tin and bake for 25 mins until set and golden. A few minutes after removing from the oven, cut the flapjacks into squares before they harden, but allow to cool completely in the tin.

Flavour variations: personally we think a simple flapjack is really quite delicious, but if you are feeling adventurous, why not try adding 75g white chocolate chips and 60g dried cranberries, or how about 75g chopped pecans and substitute 2 tablespoons of the golden syrup for 2 tablespoons of maple syrup, or for a tropical twist try adding 60g dried pineapple, 1 tablespoon rum and 50g desiccated coconut? Or try out a few of your own… the possibilities are endless!

Serves: **9 large squares**
- 300g organic unsalted butter, plus extra to grease
- 75g organic demerara sugar
- 120g organic golden syrup (6 tablespoons)
- A pinch of salt
- 250g Pimhill Organic Jumbo Oats
- 200g Pimhill Organic Porridge Oats

Chocolate Gourmet

"15 years of chocolate and still indulging – we promote quality chocolate in the whole Marches region and I am an enthusiastic connoisseur. What's not to love about proper, fine chocolate. It's made from the beans of the Theobroma cacao tree – roasted and ground to a liquor, cane sugar added, mixed to a dough and then moulded into the familiar blocks we all love. Cacao has been cultivated by many cultures for thousands of years, originally from South America where it grew wild at the time of the Olmecs. Although the Ivory Coast and Ghana are the largest producers of cocoa beans, the finest quality beans come from Venezuela, Vietnam and Madagascar. And it's made its way to me here in Shropshire!" **Janette Rowlatt**

Makes: **9-12 squares**

For the brownies:
- 150g unsalted butter
- 200g 70% dark chocolate
- 200g soft brown sugar
- 2 eggs
- A spot of vanilla essence
- 40g plain flour, sifted
- A pinch of salt
- 1 teaspoon baking powder
- 150g mixed nuts

For the chocolate drink:
- 180g dark 70% chocolate
- 500ml milk
- 50ml water
- 50ml full fat crème fraîche

Best Ever Chocolate Brownies with a Real Chocolate Drink

1 For the brownies, over a very low heat, gently melt butter and chocolate. In a separate bowl, whisk the eggs, sugar and vanilla until light and fluffy, then gently stir the melted chocolate and butter mixture in. Fold in the sifted flour, baking powder and salt. Stir in the nuts.

2 Pour into a 25x25cm oiled, lined baking tin. Bake at 180°C (160°C fan) for 45 mins or until a skewer comes out clean. Once cold, dust with icing sugar and cut into squares. Do not expect to keep these for long – they are simply scrumptious!

3 For the chocolate drink, melt the chocolate with the water in a pan over a low heat. When smooth and shiny, stir in the milk and bring to a boil for 2 mins. Remove from heat and decant into cups. Tip – Unless you have a very sweet tooth try it first, as very few people need this sweetened. Finally drop in the crème fraîche and allow it to melt.

Optional grown up version. Stir in a splash of whisky, rum or brandy whichever is your favourite, before adding the crème fraîche.

cocoa....

Simply Delicious

"We started our business on our kitchen table with one recipe, we are now in our thirteenth year and produce 14 different cakes! Our company continues to enjoy a boom as the national interest in traditional, handmade food continues to grow. Working as a husband and wife team with a small team of bakers here at the farm, we supply many trade customers and sell to a busy retail market over the internet which sends fruit cakes across the UK. We use local ingredients wherever possible; the free range eggs are from the farm over the hill, marmalade from Ludlow Food Centre and beer from Ludlow Brewing Co. If you are female and single – fruit cake can help tell your fortune – apparently sleep with a piece under your pillow after you go to a wedding – you will dream about your future husband! Ours would probably not make it under the pillow, simply too delicious…" **Milly Hunter**

Marmalade Pudding

1 Slice the cake and place half in bottom of heat proof dish. Beat the eggs, sugar and cream mixture together and dot half over the cake, repeat with cake and then the rest of the cream mixture.

2 Sprinkle some demerara sugar on top and bake in oven 180°C (160°C fan) for approx. 25 mins until the custard is set and the top is golden brown.

This pudding is delicious made with any of our cakes. Another particular favourite is made with our Apple, Pear and Beer Loaf Cake.

Serves: 6
- 1 x 500g Simply Delicious Cake Co. Marmalade Loaf Cake
- 4 eggs
- 50g demerara sugar plus extra for the top
- 250ml creme fraîche
- 200ml cream

orange

Appleteme  *mint*

"Using over 100 varieties of apples from 5 acres of orchards we keep 1000s of customers happy. We produce our juice with great attention to every detail, from picking by hand, right through to the finished product when it reaches your glass. We always mix heritage varieties to give a really deep flavour. Added to this we make the most of forgotten fruits such as the wonderful Shropshire Prune Damson, elderberries, quinces, medlars and whinberries. Blended with apples these fruits make exciting new drinks but with very traditional Shropshire flavours." **Tish Dockerty and Jane Cullen**

Apple and Damson Mojito Mocktail

1 Add some crushed ice into 2 highball glasses, pour the apple and damson juice evenly between the glasses, then add a squeeze of lime juice to each.

2 Chop, then bash the mint with a rolling pin to release the oils, thus plenty of flavour. Add the mint and cucumber to the glasses and give them a good stir.

3 Top up with the sparkling water, and add the damson concentrate ice to the top. Pop in the slices of apple, the sprig of mint and add the slice of lime to the glass. Drink and Enjoy!

Serves: 2
- 500ml Appleteme Apple and Damson juice
- ¼ of a fresh lime
- 40g cucumber, chopped into chunks
- Handful of fresh mint
- Sparkling spring water
- Handful of ice made from damson concentrate, crushed
- 2 slice of lime
- 6 slices of green apple
- 2 sprigs of mint

Hot Mulled Apple

1 Pop all the ingredients into a saucepan. Bring to a simmer and then turn down onto a low heat. Warm through for 20 mins. Taste and adjust spices, if necessary.

2 Ladle out into glasses suitable for hot drinks and serve on a crisp winter's evening to warm the soul!

Makes: 6 cups
- 750ml Appleteme Apple Juice
- 1 strip of orange peel
- 2 cloves
- 4 all spice berries
- 1 star anise
- 3cm stick of cinnamon
- 1 slice of fresh ginger

Hobsons Brewery

"Our brewery is not only famed for our award-winning beers but also our sustainable thinking. It was our choice to brew local, sourcing our ingredients from barley growers and hop farmers within 30 miles of the brewery. We brew around 200 barrels of great beer every week for our cask and bottle range, which is sold predominately within a 50 mile radius of the brewery. As the reader will know, a Hobson's choice is a free choice in which only one option is offered. As a person may refuse to take that option, the choice is therefore between taking the option or not; "take it or leave it". We suggest you drink ours – great choice!"
Kate Pearce

Saucy Postman's Pudding

1 Preheat the oven to 180°C (160°C fan). Butter and flour six individual metal pudding basins.

2 Place the prunes and the Hobsons Postman's Knock in a saucepan and bring gently to the boil. Remove from the heat and add the bicarbonate of soda. Mash the prunes with a potato masher to form a pulp. Set aside to cool slightly.

3 Place the flour, sugar, butter, eggs and vanilla essence in a food processor and process until smooth. Alternatively place all the ingredients in a bowl and beat thoroughly.

4 Add the prune mixture and mix until well combined. Pour the mixture into the prepared pudding basins then place in the centre of the oven and bake for 20-25 mins until well risen and springy to the touch.

5 Meanwhile, make the toffee sauce. Place the cream, brown sugar, Hobsons Postman's Knock and butter in a saucepan and heat gently until the sugar and butter have melted. Heat until boiling, then simmer for a few minutes, stir until smooth.

6 To serve turn out the puddings onto individual plates. Pour over some of the sauce.

Variation: This mixture can be baked in a 20cm square cake tin then cut into squares for serving. Allow an extra 5-10 mins cooking time.

Serves: 6-8
For the puddings:
- 200g ready to eat prunes, roughly chopped
- ½ teaspoon bicarbonate of soda
- 175g self-raising flour
- 175g caster sugar
- 85g butter softened
- 2 eggs, beaten
- 1 teaspoon vanilla essence

For the toffee sauce:
- 284ml double cream
- 200g soft brown sugar
- 200g unsalted butter
- 3 tablespoons Hobsons Postman's Knock

Ludlow Nut Company

"After graduating in 2005 with an MBA in Business Studies from the Open University (whilst working full time), I was determined to fulfil my ambition of starting my own food company. From humble beginnings in the basement of our home we now occupy 3,000 square feet of modern business premises. All our breakfast cereals are made by hand and we export our award winning products throughout Europe. Shropshire was a buzzing place to start our business and we have created a huge customer base in the county and beyond."
Helen Graham

Serves: 4-6

For the posset layer:
- 300ml double cream
- 75g golden caster sugar
- 1 large lemon, juice and zest

For the crunch layer:
- 40g Ludlow Nut Co. Cacao Nibs
- 100g ginger nut biscuits (broken up)
- 80g salted pretzels biscuits (broken up)
- 100g Ludlow Nut Co. Toasted Pecan and Maple Granola

For the compote layer:
- 200g strawberries, hulled and halved
- 200g raspberries
- 4 tablespoons caster sugar
- Juice of ½ a lemon
- 50ml sparkling white wine

For the vanilla cream topping:
- 350ml double cream
- 1 vanilla pod, seeds only
- 25g caster sugar
- 50g natural yoghurt

To finish:
- 70% chocolate, freshly grated
- Lemon zest, freshly grated

Ludlow Nut Co's Perfect Pecan Granola Layered Posset

1 For the posset layer, place the cream and sugar into a pan and bring to the boil slowly, stirring occasionally, boil for 3 mins, then remove from the heat and allow to cool. Add lemon juice and zest, then mix well. Pour into the bottom of your trifle glasses a small way up and allow to set for 4 hours or overnight.

2 For the crunch layer, combine all the crunch layer ingredients together in a large bowl, to make a crunchy mix.

3 For the compote layer, put all the compote ingredients (apart from the wine) into a pan and heat gently until the fruit softens and releases its juices, then simmer for 2-3 mins until it becomes a jam-like consistency, then cool. Once cool mix with a fork to break up the fruit and stir in the sparkling wine.

4 For the vanilla cream topping, whip the cream, sugar and vanilla until firm, then fold in the yoghurt. Spoon into star nozzle piping bags.

5 To build the desserts, take the set possets from the fridge, sprinkle a layer of crunchy bits on top of the posset, then spoon over the compote followed by another layer of crunch. Finish by piping the vanilla cream on top and sprinkling with more crunch, the grated chocolate and lemon zest.

granola

Ludlow Castle

"Ludlow Castle is one of the finest medieval castles still standing. With a rich and varied history it has housed kings and noblemen, prisoners, council and now food and literary festivals. Our tea rooms at the southern end of the Castle House still have the original Victorian cooking range and our site was a real tennis court in Tudor times. We serve delicious teas, and lunchtime refreshments using local suppliers but welcoming guests from all over the world who are looking for a little slice of history (or just a slice of fresh cake)." **Sonja Belchere**

Lovely Ludlow Castle Scones

1 Preheat the oven to 190°C (170°C fan). Put flour, sugar (omit sugar if making savoury scones), butter and baking powder into a mixer, blend until it reaches a breadcrumb consistency or alternatively mix by hand rubbing together with the fingers.

2 When mixed, add the eggs, and sufficient milk to mix to a soft consistency. Place on a floured work surface and roll out to about 4cm thick. Cut out the scones (take care not to twist the mixture) using a 5cm cutter and place on a greased baking tray. Cook for 10-15 mins, or until golden.

Makes: 8-12 scones
- 450g self raising flour
- 120g butter
- 60g caster sugar
- 1 teaspoon baking powder
- 2 eggs
- Milk

Flavour varieties:
- For fruit scones add 60g mixed dried fruit
- For apple and cinnamon scones add 1 teaspoon ground cinnamon and 1 diced apple (leave the skin on)
- For Shropshire blue cheese scones omit the caster sugar. Add 60g grated cheese and 1 teaspoon English mustard to the eggs

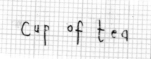

Cup of tea

Index

Wild Garlic

cobbler
Appleby's Cheshire Cheese and Apple
Cobbler, 170

cocktail
Apple and Damson Mojito Mocktail, 200
Chilton Cocktail Trio, 164
Viva Vase Vegas Cocktail, 46
Summer Rum Smoothie, 176
Pink Sunset Cocktail, 180

coconut milk
Martin McKee's Pumpkin Soup, 24
Shropshire Spice Swahili African Curry, 126

cod
Smoked Cod Loin, 116

coffee
Café Brulôt, 182
Apple Smoked Duck with Duck Confit
Croquette, 146
Easy Peasy Homemade Ice Cream, 186

cointreau
Café Brulôt, 182
Chilton Cocktail Trio, 164

confit
Apple Smoked Duck with Duck Confit
Croquette, 146
Duck, Celeriac, Damson, 132

courgette
Duo of Cherrington Farm Beef, 138

crackers
Fennel Seed Lavash Crackers, 156

cream
Café Brulôt, 182
Ludlow Nut Co's Perfect Pecan Granola
Layered Posset, 204
Smoked Cod Loin, 116
Strawberry and Lavender Pannacotta with
Basil and Violets, 174
Marmalade Pudding, 198
The Tipsy Tart's Apple and Cream Liqueur
Sponge, 180
Chocolate Salted Caramel Fondant with
Chantilly Cream, 162
Shropshire Lad Ale Braised Pork Chop, 110

croquettes
Apple Smoked Duck with Duck Confit
Croquette, 146

croutons
Warm Salad of Wood Pigeon and
Pancetta, 38

cucumber
Zingy Green Juice, 190
CSONS Chirk Ceviche, 36

curry
Masala Magic Mixed Vegetable Curry with
Cashew Nuts, 76
Shropshire Spice Swahili African Curry, 126

custard
Trifle of Madness, 188
Marmalade Pudding, 198

damson
Apple and Damson Mojito Mocktail, 200
Chilton Cocktail Trio, 164
Duck, Celeriac, Damson, 132
Pan Roast Loin of Venison, 96

dashi powder
52° North aka #FishPigPud, 60

dates
Spiced Summer Pudding Smoothie, 190

duck
Coopers Pork, Duck and Marmalade
Sausage Roll, 90
Apple Smoked Duck with Duck Confit
Croquette, 146
Duck, Celeriac, Damson, 132

duck eggs
Individual Buttercross Toad in Hole, 94
Shropshire Honey Cake, 160
Shropshire Asparagus in a Wenlock Edge
Water Tempura Batter, 14

dukka
Ful Medammes, 150

dumplings
Braised Venison and Mushroom Stew, 78

edamame beans
Happy Ayurvedic Salad, 80
52° North aka #FishPigPud, 60

eggs
Eggs Benedict, 52
Moor Farm Shop Scotch Eggs, 86

elderflower
Elderflower and Gooseberry Naked
Sponge, 168
Summer Rum Smoothie, 176

faggot
Shropshire Lamb Three Ways, 100
Rabbit and prune faggot, 130
Trio of Pork, 92

fava beans
Ful Medammes, 150

fennel
Fennel Seed Lavash Crackers, 156
Capra Nouveau, Pickled Apple, Beetroot
Carpaccio and Fennel Salad, 30
Pan Fried Sea Bream, 68
Ultimate Fennel and Heritage Tomato
Salad, 22

feta
Chilli Jam King Prawns, 44

fidget pie
Ludlow Food Centre's Shropshire Fidget
Pie, 70

fillet
Fillet of Harper Beef with a Café de Paris
Butter, 104
Beef with Mushroom in Oyster Sauce, 122

fish
Barkworths Saint-Pierre Bouillabaisse, 58
Pickled Fillet of Red Mullet, 32
CSONS Chirk Ceviche, 36
Pan Fried Sea Bream, 68
Seared Scallops, Pork Belly, Pork
Scratchings and Apple Emulsion, 26
Monkfish Cheeks with a Soy Caramel
Glaze, Pork Bon Bons and Apple Miso
Purée, 46
52° North aka #FishPigPud, 60
Smoked Cod Loin, 116
Fish Pie Tartlet, 40

flapjacks
Pimhill Organic Flapjacks, 194

flat bread
CSONS Chirk Ceviche, 36

flour
Fennel Seed Lavash Crackers, 156

flowers
Strawberry and Lavender Pannacotta
with Basil and Violets, 174

fondant
Chocolate Salted Caramel Fondant with
Chantilly Cream, 162

fondue
Marches Fondue, 152

fruit
Trifle of Madness, 188

gammon
Ludlow Food Centre's Shropshire Fidget
Pie, 70

Directory

A Nice Slice of Cake
Beautiful handmade delights created using the best natural ingredients.
www.anicesliceofcake.weebly.com
anicesliceofcake@yahoo.co.uk
07815 136020
Whitchurch, SY13 1ES

Acton Scott Historic Working Farm
The UK's number one Victorian attraction, a great day out for the whole family.
www.actonscottmuseum.com
01694 781307
Wenlock Lodge, Acton Scott, Church Stretton, SY6 6QN

The Albright Hussey Manor Hotel
16th Century moated manor hotel with 26 ensuite rooms and restaurant.
www.albrighthussey.co.uk
info@albrighthussey.co.uk
01939 290571
Broad Oak, Shrewsbury, SY4 3AF

Apley Farm Shop
Taste, discover, enjoy. So much more than a farm shop.
www.apleyfarmshop.co.uk
general.manager@apleyfarmshop.co.uk
01952 730345
Norton, TF11 9EF

Applebys
Farmers and cheesemakers producing award winning Cheshire cheese since 1952.
www.applebyscheese.co.uk
dairy@applebyscheese.co.uk
01948 840221 / 07932 254718
Hawkstone Abbey Farm, Marchamley, Shrewsbury, SY4 5LN

Appleteme
We press and blend heritage apple varieties for depth of flavour.
www.appleteme.com
tish@appleteme.com / jane@appleteme.com
07985 218727 / 07970 433853
Tickmore, Brimfield Common, Ludlow, SY8 4NZ

The Armoury
The Armoury is a truly impressive space with lovely windows looking over the River Severn.
www.brunningandprice.co.uk/armoury
armoury@brunningandprice.co.uk
01743 340525
Victoria Quay, Victoria Avenue, Shrewsbury, SY1 1HH

Aroma Tea & Coffee Merchants
Roasting ethical and unique coffee from around the world since 1981.
www.aroma-coffee.co.uk
sales@aroma-coffee.co.uk
Retail 01743 367598 Trade 01743 457567
Shop – 8a St Mary's Place, Shrewsbury, SY1 1DZ
Roastery – 4 Hotspur Park, Shrewsbury, SY1 3FB

Bacheldre Watermill
Artisan millers of award winning stone ground flours.
www.bacheldremill.co.uk
info@bacheldremill.co.uk
01588 620489
Churchstoke, Montgomery, SY15 6TE

Bank House B&B (@BankHouseBnB)
Country house comfort for groups of up to 14 for walking, cycling, yoga, art, etc.
www.bishopscastlebedandbreakfast.co.uk
bookings@bishopscastlebedandbreakfast.co.uk
01588 630026 / 07712 010525
Bank House, 4 High Street, Bishop's Castle, SY9 5BQ

Barkworths Seafoods Ltd
Quality fishmongers and seafood suppliers with seafood bar.
www.barkworths.co.uk
info@barkworths.co.uk
01743 352138
16-17 Market Hall, Shrewsbury, SY1 1HQ

Battlefield 1403 Ltd
Farm shop, butchery, deli and café sited on the historic Battlefield of Shrewsbury.
www.battlefield1403.com
info@battlefield1403.com
01939 210905
Upper Battlefield, Shrewsbury, SY4 3DB

Bennett & Dunn Ltd
Artisan producers of cold pressed rapeseed oil.
www.bennettanddunn.co.uk
info@bennettanddunn.co.uk
07474 887453
Shipley

Bistro 7 of Ludlow
Beautiful bistro in lovely Ludlow, cooking up delicious homemade food with local ingredients.
www.bistro7ofludlow.co.uk
hello@bistro7ofludlow.co.uk
01584 877412
7 Corve Street, Ludlow, SY8 1DB

Brock Hall Farm Dairy
Artisan goats cheese from own herd of Saanen goats.
www.brockhallfarm.com
01746 862533
Chelmarsh, Bridgnorth, WV16 6QA

Brompton Cookery School
Cookery school with farmhouse B&B, the perfect environment to develop your practical culinary skills.
www.bromptoncookeryschool.co.uk
info@bromptoncookeryschool.co.uk
01743 761629
Upper Farm, Brompton Cross Houses, SY5 6LE

Butterbelle
Artisan nut butters made with all natural ingredients.
www.butterbelle.co.uk
info@butterbelle.co.uk
07964 049402
Brookside House, Vicarage Drive, Shifnal, TF11 9AE

Buttercross Farm Foods Ltd
Artisan pork, bacon and ham curers, supplying discerning retailers, restaurants and manufacturers.
www.buttercross.com
info@buttercross.com
01630 656670
Shiffords Grange Farm, Red Bull, Market Drayton, TF9 2QS

Chef in the Wood
Events caterer serving homemade chef prepared food from a pop-up kitchen.
www.chefinthewood.co.uk
info@chefinthewood.co.uk
07793 461067
Brownlow Cottage, Brown Moss, Whitchurch, SY13 4BU

Chilton Liqueurs
Damson gin made with Shropshire Prune damsons and Greenalls Gin.
www.chiltondamsongin.co.uk
sales@chiltondamsongin.com
01588 650516
Myndtown Cottage, Lydbury North, SY7 8BL

Chocolate Gourmet
Specialist retailer of quality truffles, single bean and origin bars.
www.chocolategourmet.co.uk
sales@chocolategourmet.co.uk
01584 879332 / 01743 343477
16 Castle Street, Ludlow, SY8 1AT /
72 Wyle Cop, Shrewsbury, SY1 1UX

Churncote Farm Shop, Butchery & Café
Producing our own farm reared meats and produce.
www.churncote.co.uk
info@churncote.co.uk
01743 851913
Welshpool Road, Bicton Heath, Shrewsbury, SY3 5EB

The Clive
Award winning restaurant with rooms.
www.theclive.co.uk
info@theclive.co.uk
01584 856565
Bromfield, Ludlow, SY8 2JR

The Coach & Horses
16th century coaching inn serving good quality home cooked food using the best of Shropshire's produce.
www.odleyinns.co.uk/coach-horses
coach@odley.co.uk
01743 365661
Swan Hill, Shrewsbury, SY1 1NF

Cooking Like Cleopatra
The soul of Egyptian cuisine, providing food tours, cultural team development, cooking events and culinary delights.
www.cooking-like-cleopatra.com
marina@cooking-like-cleopatra.com
07958 629220
Ludlow, SY8 1LP

Coopers Gourmet Sausage Rolls
Gourmet sausage rolls made with the finest local ingredients.
www.coopers-sausage-rolls.co.uk
sales@coopers-sausage-rolls.com
01743 441811
Unit 10 Shropshire Food Enterprise Centre, Vanguard Way, Battlefield, Shrewsbury, SY1 3TG

Crows (Agricultural Ltd)
Producer of pedigree Shropshire sheep.
sarah.crow123@gmail.com
07989 970840
The Old Forge, Little Longnor, Nr Dorrington, Shrewsbury, SY5 7QF

CSONS
A café and restaurant specialising in locally sourced, globally inspired seasonal food and drink.
www.csons-shrewsbury.co.uk
eat@csons-shrewsbury.co.uk
01743 272709
8 Milk Street, Shrewsbury, SY1 1SZ

Fordhall Organic Farm
A 140 acre community owned organic farm with café, shop and free trails in the picturesque Tern Valley.
www.fordhallfarm.com
project@fordhallfarm.com
01630 638696
Tern Hill Road, Market Drayton, TF9 3PS

The Foundry
Level 2 Theatre Severn restaurant with great river views and food.
www.the-foundry.info
enquiries@the-foundry.info
01743 272767
Level 2 Theatre Severn, Frankwell Quay, Shrewsbury, SY3 8FT

Granary Grill & Deli
A first class food destination at stately home, Weston Park.
www.granarygrill.com
enquiries@weston-park.com
01952 852107
Weston Park, Weston-under-Lizard, Nr Shifnal, TF11 8LE

Great Berwick Organics
Suppliers of organic, pasture fed, 35 day dry aged Longhorn beef.
www.longhornbeef.co.uk
greatberwick@googlemail.com
01743 351939
Great Berwick Farm, Berwick Road, Shrewsbury, SY4 3HS

Great Ness Oil Ltd
Producers of cold pressed extra virgin rapeseed oil and infusions.
www.greatnessoil.co.uk
info@greatnessoil.co.uk
01939 261384
The Old Parsonage, Little Ness, Shrewsbury, SY4 2LG

Green Fields Farm Shop
The home of local food.
www.greenfieldsonline.co.uk
info@greenfieldsonline.co.uk
01952 677345 / 01952 200696
Station Road, Donnington, Telford, TF2 8JY / Lakeside Plant Centre, Priorslee, Telford, TF2 9UR

Hadley Park House
Tastefully extended Georgian manor house, with strong focus on local sourcing.
www.hadleypark.co.uk
info@hadleypark.co.uk
01952 677269
Hadley Park East, Telford, TF1 6QJ

The Happy Boho
Lifestyle and well-being blog, scattered with resources to inspire you to live a happier, healthier, balanced life.
www.happyboho.com

Harper Adams University
www.harper-adams.ac.uk
01952 820280
Newport, TF10 8NB

Heathers Harvest
Award winning artisan chutneys, jams and marmalades.
www.heathers-harvest.co.uk
heather@heathers-harvest.co.uk
01743 588437 / 07791 953369
Unit 22 Monkmoor Farm Estate, Monkmoor Road, Shrewsbury, SY2 5TL

Henry Tudor House
Classic cuisine with modern twists and flamboyant flavours.
www.henrytudorhouse.com
hello@henrytudorhouse.com
01743 361666
Barracks Passage, Shrewsbury, SY1 1XA

Hobsons Brewery
Shropshire brewer famed for award-winning beers and sustainable thinking.
www.hobsons-brewery.co.uk
beer@hobsons-brewery.co.uk
01299 270837
Newhouse Farm, Tenbury Road, Cleobury Mortimer, DY14 8RD

Hopton House B&B
A relaxing luxury B&B in the beautiful Shropshire Hills.
www.shropshirebreakfast.co.uk
karen@shropshirebreakfast.com
Hopton House, Hopton Heath, Craven Arms, SY7 0QD

House of the Rising Sun
Modern Australian cuisine with Pacific Rim flavours, using local produce.
www.hotrs.co.uk
info@hotrs.co.uk
01743 588040
18 Butcher Row, Shrewsbury, SY1 1UW

The Hundred House
Characterful and quirky pub with rooms, beautiful gardens and great food.
www.hundredhouse.co.uk
reservations@hundredhouse.co.uk
01952 580240
Norton, Telford, Ironbridge, TF11 9EE

The Ironbridge Catering Company
BBQ, big pan and event caterer with a difference.
www.ironbridgecatering.co.uk
sales@ironbridgecatering.co.uk
07980 148268
Unit 8 St Georges Industrial Estate, Donnington, TF2 7QZ

Katie's Kids Kitchen
Children cookery school.
www.katieskidskitchen.co.uk
katieskidskitchen@gmail.com
07971 499359
3 Pools Cottages, Annscroft, Shrewsbury, SY5 5AX

Kerry Vale Vineyard
Family run vineyard, with wine café and shop.
www.kerryvalevineyard.co.uk
info@kerryvalevineyard.co.uk
01588 620627
Pentreheyling, Churchstoke, SY15 6HU

King & Thai Restaurant
Nationally awarded neighbourhood restaurant specialising in Thai cuisine fusing locally sourced ingredients.
www.kingandthai.co.uk
hello@kingandthai.co.uk
01952 882004
Avenue Road, Nr Broseley, TF12 5DL

Ludlow Brewing Co. Ltd
Producing high quality ales from a stunningly converted railway shed, in the heart of Ludlow.
www.theludlowbrewingcompany.co.uk
beer@theludlowbrewingcompany.co.uk
01584 873291
The Railway Shed, Station Drive, Ludlow, SY8 2PQ

Ludlow Castle
The finest of medieval ruined castles in glorious Shropshire countryside.
www.ludlowcastle.com
info@ludlowcastle.com
01584 874465
Castle Square, Ludlow, SY8 1AY

Ludlow Food Centre
Britain's best food hall 2014 and best farm shop 2013.
www.ludlowfoodcentre.co.uk
greatfood@ludlowfoodcentre.co.uk
01584 856000
Bromfield, Ludlow, SY8 2JR

Ludlow Food Festival
A festival celebrating food and drink from Ludlow and the Marches based inside Ludlow Castle, 2nd weekend in May and September.
www.foodfestival.co.uk
info@foodfestival.co.uk
Unit 12, The Business Quarter, Eco Park Road, Ludlow, SY8 1FD

The Ludlow Nut Co. Ltd
Producers of breakfast cereals, snack bars, nuts, dried fruits and confectionery.
www.ludlownutco.co.uk
sales@ludlownutco.co.uk
01584 876512
Unit 19-20, Rural Enterprise Centre, Eco Park Road, Ludlow, SY8 1NG

Ludlow Vineyard & Distillery
Distillers of apple and grape brandy, eau de vie and whisky.
www.ludlowdistillery.co.uk
distillery@ludlowdistillery.co.uk
01584 823356
Wainbridge House, Clee St Margaret, Craven Arms, SY7 9DT

Masala Magic
Teaching authentic Indian cooking and creating unique spice blends for you.
www.masalamagic.kitchen
lajina@masalamagic.kitchen
01952 303031 / 07866 969993
Telford Enterprise Hub, Hadley Park East, Telford, TF1 6QJ

Maynard's Farm Bacon Ltd
Artisan bacon and gammon curers and traditional sausage producers.
www.maynardsfarm.co.uk
sales@maynardsfarm.co.uk
01948 840252
Hough Farm, Weston-under-Redcastle, Shrewsbury, SY4 5 LR

Merangz Ltd
Slow baked traditional Swiss meringues with a crisp shell and soft centre.
www.merangz.co.uk
hello@merangz.co.uk
01745 443864
Units 11-12 Shropshire Food Enterprise Centre, Vanguard Way, Shrewsbury, SY1 3TG

Mikes Homemade
Producers of award winning homemade chutney, pickles, preserves, marmalade, mustard, sauces and honey.
www.mikeshomemade.co.uk
mike@mikeshomemade.co.uk
01785 284767 / 07791 699347
Fairview, Newport Road, Woodseaves, ST20 0NP

Momo·No·Ki Ramen Noodle Bar
#ASIANSOULFOOD – done properly.
www.momonoki.co.uk
kirstie@momonoki.co.uk / chris@momonoki.co.uk
01743 281770
19 Abbey Foregate, Shrewsbury, SY2 6AE

Moor Farm Shop & Tea Room
Family run farm, shop and tea room selling as much homemade and local produce as possible.
www.moorfarmshop.co.uk
shop@moorfarmshop.co.uk
01939 262632
Moor Farm, Ruyton Road, Baschurch, Shrewsbury, SY4 2BA

Moyden's Handmade Cheese
Award winning artisan cheeses that are the essence of Shropshire.
www.mrmoyden.com
mrmoyden@live.co.uk
01630 639796
The Creamery, Lockley Villa Farm, Wistanswick, Market Drayton, TF9 2AY

Netherton Foundry
Makers and purveyors of classic cookware.
www.netherton-foundry.co.uk
sales@netherton-foundry.co.uk
01746 862781
Unit 6, Netherton Workshops, New Road, Highley, WV16 6NN

Old Downton Lodge
Luxury restaurant with rooms located in the Downton Gorge site of special scientific interest.
www.olddowntonlodge.com
bookings@olddowntonlodge.com
01568 771826
Downton on the Rock, Nr Ludlow, SY8 2HU

Olive Tree at Holiday Inn Telford / Ironbridge
A unique hotel-based restaurant serving fresh,
home-made cuisine.
01952 527000
St Quentin Gate, Telford, TF3 4EH
www.holidayinntelford.com

The Pheasant at Neenton
Superb Shropshire food in a real country pub owned
by the community.
www.pheasantatneenton.co.uk
info@pheasantatneenton.co.uk
01746 787955
Pheasant Inn, Neenton, Bridgnorth, WV16 6RJ

Pimhill Farm
Growing, milling and hand packing organic wheat
and oat products.
www.pimhill.co.uk
sales@pimhill.co.uk
01939 291310
Harmer Hill, Shrewsbury, SY4 3DY

Raven Hotel (Wenlock) Ltd
Fine dining restaurant and independent hotel in
historic Much Wenlock.
www.ravenhotel.com
enquiry@ravenhotel.com
01952 727251
Much Wenlock, TF13 6EN

Marketplace at The Raven
Fresh fish, baked goods and top quality, often unusual,
fruit and vegetables.
www.ravenhotel.com
enquiry@ravenhotel.com
01952 727251
The Cart Shed, The Raven Hotel, Much Wenlock, TF13 6EN

Rowlands & Co. (Shrewsbury) Ltd
Wholesaler of fresh and dried products to the trade.
www.rowlandsltd.co.uk
sales@rowlandsltd.co.uk
01743 462244
Rowlands Fresh Produce ltd, 9 Knights Way,
Battlefields Enterprise Park, Shrewsbury, SY1 3AB

Shrewsbury College
Further education college in Shrewsbury with a renowned
hospitality and catering department.
www.shrewsbury.ac.uk
danielg@shrewsbury.ac.uk
01743 342491
Shrewsbury College, London Road, Shrewsbury, SY2 6PR

Shrewsbury Flower Show
Flowers, fireworks and fun for all the Family – held in the
Quarry in August.
www.shrewsburyflowershow.org.uk
info@shrewsburyflowershow.org.uk
01743 234050
Shropshire Horticultural Society, Quarry Lodge,
Shrewsbury, SY1 1RN

Shrewsbury Food Festival
A festival of food and drink, with local craft, live music and
tons of family entertainment, on the last weekend of June.
www.shrewsburyfoodfestival.co.uk
beth@shrewsburyfoodfestival.co.uk
01952 432175

The Shropshire Ice Cream Company
Artisan producer of luxury ice cream and sorbets using
locally sourced ingredients.
www.shropshireicecream.co.uk
enquiries@shropshireicecream.co.uk
07580 632130
Unit 53, Business Development Centre, Stafford Park 4,
Telford, TF3 3BA

The Shropshire Spice Co. Ltd
Small family owned company producing quality stuffing mixes,
world blend spice mixes – great store cupboard essentials.
www.shropshire-spice.co.uk
office@shropshire-spice.co.uk
01588 640100
The Green Ind Est, Clun, Craven Arms, SY7 8LG

The Shropshire Spirit Co.
Fabulously Salopian spirits.
www.shropshirespritco.co.uk
jcrone@shropshirespritco.co.uk
07794 004875
Unit 11C, M54 Space Centre, Halesfield 8, TF7 4QN

Shropshire's Own
Award winning village shop with a passion for great
local food!
www.shropshiresown.co.uk
info@shropshiresown.co.uk
01743 860459
Longden Post Office, Shrewsbury Road,
Longden, SY5 8EX

The Simply Delicious Cake Co.
Handmade cakes made in the traditional way.
www.simplydeliciouscakes.co.uk
info@simplydeliciouscakes.co.uk
01584 823679
Moor Farm, Cleedownton, Ludlow, SY8 3EG

Swifts (Richard C. Swift Ltd)
Craft baker of artisan breads.
www.swifts.bakery.co.uk / www.bread2bake.co.uk
bread2bake12@gmail.com
01584 838415
Unit 18, Ludlow Eco Park, Ludlow, SY8 1FF

Sytch Farm Studios
Hand thrown ceramics and hand crafted wooden serving
and chopping boards, created to be used with food.
www.sytchfarmstudios.co.uk
sytchfarmstudios@gmail.com
01743 718908
Sytch Farm, Dorrington, Shrewsbury, SY5 7LL

Taste of Shrewsbury Ltd
Sandwich, juice bar, coffee shop, takeaway or eat in facilities.
taste.of.shrewsbury@btconnect.com
01743 359783
70 Mardol, Shrewsbury, SY1 1PZ

Thank Goodness Ltd
Producing gourmet hand-made vegetarian foods, including our Shroppie Pie.
www.thankgoodnessltd.com
enquiries@thankgoodnessltd.com
01952 813767
2, Granville Avenue, Newport, TF10 7DX

The Tipsy Tart
Luscious Liqueurs – fabulously fruity, funky and fun.
www.thetipsytart.co.uk
elizabeth@thetipsytart.co.uk
01584 872078
Ludlow

Toot Sweets Chocolates
Multi award winning handmade chocolates using high quality single origin chocolate and Shropshire ingredients.
www.tootsweetschcolates.co.uk
julia@tootsweetschocolates.co.uk
07814 113156
Unit 8, The Market Hall, Claremont Street, Shrewsbury, SY3 8N

Treflach Farm
Family farm and CIC providing education about farming, food production and the environment; part-funded through the sale of tasty homemade pies.
www.treflachfarm.co.uk
info@treflachfarm.co.uk
01691 654321
Treflach Farm, Oswestry, SY10 9HX

Wenlock Edge Farm
Artisan bacon curers and producers of speciality pork products.
www.wenlockedgefarm.co.uk
peter@wenlockedgefarm.co.uk
01694 771893
Edge House, East Wall, Much Wenlock, TF13 6DU

Wenlock Spring Water
Shropshire based premium bottled water producer.
www.wenlockspring.co.uk
info@wenlockspring.co.uk
01694 781277
Wolverton, Church Stretton, SY6 6RR

White Hart, Ironbridge
Modern styled pub and rooms, café bar by day, grown up restaurant and bar every evening.
www.whitehartironbridge.com
info@whitehartironbridge.com
01952 432901
Wharfage, Ironbridge, TF8 7AW

Willo Game
Supplier of wild game to wholesalers, retailers, food service and the public.
www.willogame.co.uk
enquiries@willogame.co.uk
01588 650119
Mid Shires Foods, Shuttocks Wood, Norbury, SY9 5EA

The Wood Brewery Ltd
Brewers of draught and bottled beers including Shropshire Lad and Lass.
www.woodbrewery.co.uk
ewood@woodbrewery.co.uk
01588 672523
Wistanstow, Craven Arms, SY7 8DG

Wroxeter Roman Vineyard Ltd
Growers and producers of English wine and cider.
www.wroxetervineyard.co.uk
shop@wroxetervineyard.co.uk
01743 761888
Wroxeter, Shrewsbury, SY5 6PQ

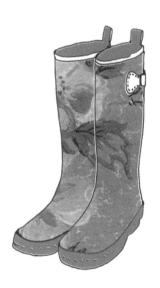

Conversion table

Weights	Metric Imperial
10g	½oz
20g	¾oz
25g	1oz
40g	1½oz
50g	2oz
60g	2½oz
75g	3oz
110g	4oz
125g	4½oz
150g	5oz
175g	6oz
200g	7oz
225g	8oz
250g	9oz
275g	10oz
350g	12oz
450g	1lb
900g	2lb

Dimensions	Metric Imperial
3mm	inch
5mm	¼ inch
1cm	½ inch
2cm	¾ inch
2.5cm	1 inch
3cm	1¼ inch
4cm	1½ inch
5cm	2 inch
6cm	2½ inch
7.5cm	3 inch
10cm	4 inch
13cm	5 inch
15cm	6 inch
18cm	7 inch
20cm	8 inch
23cm	9 inch
25.5cm	10 inch
28cm	11 inch
30cm	12 inch

Volume	Metric Imperial
55ml	2 fl oz
75ml	3 fl oz
150ml	5 fl oz (¼ pint)
275ml	10 fl oz (½ pint)
570ml	1 pint
725ml	1 ¼ pint
1 litre	1 ¾ pint
1.2 litre	2 pint
1.5 litre	2½ pint

Oven Temperatures

°C	°F	Gas Mark
140°C	275°F	1
150°C	300°F	2
170°C	325°F	3
180°C	350°F	4
190°C	375°F	5
200°C	400°F	6
220°C	425°F	7
230°C	450°F	8
240°C	475°F	9

NB. All are approximate conversions, which have been rounded for ease. Never mix metric and imperial measures in one recipe.

A little mention

Special thanks go to...

Pearl Taylor, Stephen and Linda Wild for their eagle eyes.

Tiger Helicopters for taking us up, up and away.

Recipe credits

Shropshire Asparagus in a Wenlock Spring Tempura
by Andy Link at The Riverside Inn www.theriversideinn.org

Ultimate Fennel and Heritage Tomato Salad
by Loopy Folkes laurafolkes@gmail.com

Capra Nouveau, Pickled Apple, Beetroot Carpaccio and Fennel Salad
by Andy Link at The Riverside Inn www.theriversideinn.org

Pickled Fillet of Red Mullet
by Dan Smith at the Mytton and Mermaid www.myttonandmermaid.co.uk

Warm Salad of Wood Pigeon and Pancetta
by Lesley Mackley

Wrekin Salad
by Andy Link at The Riverside Inn www.theriversideinn.org

Shropshire Sourdough
from "Born and Bread" by Robert Swift

Pan Fried Sea Bream
by Ian Matfin

Individual Buttercross Toad in Hole
by Andy Link at The Riverside Inn www.theriversideinn.org

Pan Roast Loin of Venison
by Andy Link at The Riverside Inn www.theriversideinn.org

Shropshire Lad Ale Braised Pork Chop
by Andy Link at The Riverside Inn www.theriversideinn.org

Pan Roast Breast of Shropshire Pheasant, wrapped in Wenlock Edge Prosciutto
by Andy Link at The Riverside Inn www.theriversideinn.org

Ful Medammes – a hearty broad bean stew – the Shropshire way
from "Delicious Dukka Recipes" by Cooking Like Cleopatra

Marches Fondue
by Lesley Mackley

Fennel Seed Lavash Crackers
by Andy Link at The Riverside Inn www.theriversideinn.org

Chilton Cocktail Trio
by Felix Cohen www.manhattansproject.com

Strawberry and Lavender Pannacotta with Basil and Violets
by Paul Crowe @chefpaulcrowe

Bank House Healthy Drink Duo
by Penny Horner at Meadowlark Yoga, Edinburgh and www.intrepidlyrawsome.com

Walnut and Maple Butter Tartlet with Ginger and Honey Ice Cream
by Andy Link at The Riverside Inn www.theriversideinn.org

Saucy Postman's Pudding
by Deborah Powell from Hobsons Funkie Food and Ale Cook Book

fork   knife   spoon